LET THE CHILDREN SING

Let the Children Sing

Kathryn S. Wright

A CROSSROAD BOOK
The Seabury Press, NEW YORK

The Seabury Press
815 Second Avenue
New York, N.Y. 10017

Copyright © 1975 The Seabury Press, Inc.
Designed by Paula Wiener
Printed in the United States of America

Library of Congress Cataloging in Publication Data
Wright, Kathryn S.
  Let the childen sing.
  "A Crossroad book."
  1. Music in religious education.   I. Title.
BV1534.8.W74   268'.432   73-17915
ISBN 0-8164-0256-6

To all singing children everywhere
whether one year old or one hundred and one

For God the Father Almighty
plays upon the harp of
stupendous magnitude and melody.

—Christopher Smart

Contents

Preface of Praise

Thanks be to God for making music possible, and to composers for giving it birth.

Thanks to those churches whose life has contributed to the making of this book, but especially to the First Presbyterian Church of Port Jervis, New York, where the fellowship of music led by the Reverend Richard Avery and the choir director, Donald Marsh, inspired me to write it.

Thanks to all who have shared news of music in their respective churches: Mrs. John Bruére of Cleveland, Ohio; Barbara Hampton, director of music at the University Heights Presbyterian Church in the Bronx, New York City; the Reverend Ben Jacobson, minister of Christian education at the New York Avenue Presbyterian Church in Washington, and Stephen Prussing, director of the choir; Dr. Eugene Laubach of the Riverside Church in New York, and Fred Swann, organist and director of the choir; Bruce Nehring, organist and choir director in El Paso,

Texas; Father Lew O'Neil, S. J., formerly associated with the St. Stephens Mission in Wyoming; the Reverend George Pera of Greenwich, Connecticut, and Julia Totten, director of Christian education; the Reverend Roger Shoup at the Calvary Presbyterian Church in Cleveland.

Thanks to the families and teachers who have shared their musical experience and their photographs;

to Jon Whatson of the Nottingham Playhouse in England, for his help in securing permission to quote three poems by children;

to the Rev. James Bryden of Alexandria, Virginia, for the factual story about Lincoln and the two boys;

to Michael Feist, for permission to use the photograph of the three barefoot "angels";

to Proclamation Productions, for their response to innumerable queries and for permission to quote the songs by Richard K. Avery and Donald S. Marsh.

to the staff of the Port Jervis Free Library for their assistance in tracking down elusive information.

LET THE CHILDREN SING

1
Rhythm and Relationship

W H E N children sing, they are happy because music is a part of being alive, and singing is the most personal expression of it. The instrument is one's own body animated by one's own breath, and only God, they say, can come closer to us than that. How quaint it is that like a traveling orchestra with an organ and amplifier, we carry our own string section, loud speaker, and bellows right along with us wherever we go. Yes, even drums, if you include clapping hands, stamping feet, and thumping chests. The special wonder of it is that *our* equipment is built into our bodies at birth and so, barring illness, is always available.

Have you ever watched the mystery of an infant learning to make his first sounds other than crying? As an adoring aunt, I leaned over my nephew's crib time and time again during his early months to verify the sounds I thought I heard. I had expected a gurgle or two, perhaps the sound "Coo" with a "C," but here he was, uttering "Goo" with a "G," preceded by a long-drawn "Ah," and both syllables so sweetly sustained as to be definitely musical. Did I imagine that the "G" was soft rather than hard, like the "ch" sound in the Hebrew word for "breath"? Or in the German word for "I-me-myself"? In any case, what I heard was to me a song, and it went something like this:

First Verse (experimentally):
    Ah-goo
    Ah-gooo
    Ah-goooo!
       Chorus: A tentative smile
Second Verse (confidently):
    Repeat above with variations, rising to the finale fortissimo with high kicks of great vigor and joy.
       Chorus: A smile of ecstasy

Do you catch the rhythm of the song? Iambic for the lyrics, wouldn't you say—one short, one long? And possibly notes in ⅜ time with a good long hold on the last one. Professional linguists and musicians may not agree with my findings, but if the reader wants to enjoy his infant friends with heightened awareness, I do recommend cribside auditions, preferably without a tape recorder. Being busy with a gadget could short-circuit your love for the child, which is an important part of his song. He will know the difference between a warm experience and a scientific experiment, so why not print the music in your own mind and heart? You can jot it down later if you must.

You may find quite different sounds and a different beat, but "words" and beat will be there, the sounds more obvious than the rhythm perhaps, but you will hear both if you persist. Life is full of rhythm—the orbit of a planet, spring and fall, night and day, family comings and goings, our very breathing and the beating of our hearts. Perhaps the first stimulus an unborn child receives is the rhythm of a heartbeat, his own as well as his mother's. This may be one of the reasons why music can bring joy. It puts us in touch with a basic element in life itself.

There is a kind of music even in the steady beat of water from a garden spray, as I learned one day when my nephew "Littlejohn" discovered the joy of playing in it. Head back, eyes closed, he gave himself to the fountain, dancing a rhythm of delight.

Our choir director, Don Marsh, tells of a veritable chorus of garden sprays he saw during a workshop in the country. They were turning in various speeds about the open "campus," and children went leaping from one sprinkler to another, trying to synchronize their movements with the rhythm of the water. At first their goal seemed to be to stay dry, later, to dare to get wet. In any case, the air was filled with laughter and excitement in one grand joyous movement of children and fountains at play.

Or take a stairway. It can lead to music too. When Littlejohn was making his transition from the crawl to the walk, he used the stairs like the keyboard of a piano, gleefully "playing" every note from top to bottom like a scale. He enjoyed the ascending and descending movement over and over again, one step at a time, sitting briefly on each before hoisting himself up or letting himself down. Sometimes the tempo would vary from *andante* to *allegro,* and the mood from *con spirito* to *largo.* If he felt the need of a rest, he would take it, and just sit there. But at his most brilliant, in his most purple passages so to speak, he moved along confidently with a little humming sound worthy of Winnie the Pooh, yet entirely his own. His own personal hum to joy.

Out of my own joy at the time I wrote these lines to commemorate his journey into rhythm:

> *Joy Ride for Johnny*
> I go downstairs every morning
> I go upstairs every night
> but now and then
> I do it again
> all through the day
> in a better way:
>
> I go   up
>   up   and
>   and   down
>   down and
> simply for the fun of it.
>
> Sometimes I am a monkey
> climbing a monkey tree
> sometimes I am a sailor
> climbing a ship at sea.
>
> One day I was Daddy
> hunting for a bear,
> then I was a camel
> humping here and there.
>
> Last night I was Momee
> going to a ball,
> tomorrow I may be
> nothing grand at all.

At the risk of letting my nephew monopolize this chapter, here is one more adventure with him to show how relationship can be shared through rhythm. I was playing the piano for my own amusement and he was sitting on the couch where I had left him with nothing at all to do, his chubby legs straight out in front of him. Suddenly I realized that he was trying to rock back and forth in time with the music, but he was having trouble because the beat was not an easy one to follow. He was trying hard to relate to what was going on but the music was not his kind. It ignored him. What a way to treat a friend! I closed the score and tried to let notes come off my hands as they would to match what *he* was doing.

> *DOWN* to the toes and / BACK up to sit-sit
> *ONE*-2 and 3 and 4 / *ONE*-2 and 3-4
> *HARD* on the first beat/ FOUR-four the rhy-thm
> KEEP right on go-o-ing/ KEEP right ON!

He noticed the difference immediately and responded with enthusiasm. It was not long before we had a piece of music custombuilt for him. I call it "His Song," although there are no words to it and it is not his alone, for other children have moved to its rhythm while walking, running, skipping, hopping, jumping, marching. They say that a child's attention-span is as many minutes long as he is years old. It was not so with Johnny. He was only about a year old but the song held his attention for five minutes and more. Rocking happily back and forth to a rhythm he could relate to, he was intensely in touch with life and saying so in his own way.

Some say that rhythm has developed from man's instinctive urge to express his inner experience and feelings in muscular movements. With their permission I am including here the story of an experience in New Mexico shared by our minister Richard Avery, and choirmaster

Donald Marsh on the day they visited an Indian pueblo
for an annual celebration, the only religious ceremonial
dance which outsiders are permitted to attend. A choir
of one hundred voices led the singing and a group of
three hundred people took part in the dancing, one hundred
of whom were children. Several were women of eighty
years or more. With the help of a drummer, they danced
from ten in the morning until dusk as a fervent prayer
for good crops.

The power of the simple step-step-step rhythm held the
circle of dancers together in a remarkable way. Even
when there was an occasional pause, like a rest in music
but without any apparent warning signal, none of the
three hundred got out of step or out of line. When some
of the young boys began to act up—glaring, jabbering,
and even punching each other—they still maintained the
constant movement with their feet, never once breaking
rhythm. A dance that may have had its roots in a spontaneous response long ago had perhaps been repeated so
many times as a commonly accepted value that it cannot
be broken without a command from the chief to the
entire group. Certainly not by the in-fighting of a few
youthful individuals.

The variety in singing that is possible through differences
in rhythm is also a source of enjoyment and renewal.
Monotony is no problem when you can offer children the
flowing rhythm of Jacqueline McNair's Hawaiian carol
"Al-le-lu!" and the vigorous beat of "The Old Is New"
by Lloyd Pfautsch, or the gentle simplicity of "The Great
Commandment" by Jane Marshall.

The children in the choirs of our church in Port Jervis,
New York, have enjoyed all these songs. They expect
variety in rhythm and would be disappointed without it,
having had the considerable privilege of singing "hot off
the griddle" the "proclamation" music composed by their

own minister and choir conductor, the Avery and Marsh team. They have learned to catch a tune and a mood along with the rhythm, whether it is the joyous bounce of "Here We Go A-Caroling" or the slow haunting "Love Them Now" with its plea for understanding the unlovely people in the world.

A member of another church where the Proclamation music is used tells me the favorite song of the children there is the Epiphany Carol, "Take Time." This is not surprising, for with its steady accent on the first and third beats, you can almost *see* the camels stalking along with the Wise Men aboard. And if the "ching" of finger cymbals can be added on the rests as the composers suggest, the effect of mystery and adventure can be truly spine-tingling.

In contemporary music, the rest is often used creatively. In "Hey! Hey! Anybody listening?" one rest of an entire measure plus two beats in the next sharpens the point of the song. And at the end of the song, following the words "anybody listening?" the music is left unfinished, the question left hanging for the audience to answer.

This song and many others that the children sing we also sing together in the spirit of family fellowship our church richly enjoys. People of all ages have learned to be at home with both the old and the new tunes for the "Doxology" and the "Gloria Patri" so that with only a few notes the organist can signal which version has been chosen for that day and the worshipers can follow through without a printed program. This makes it possible to have a flexible service. Our regular hymnal is used, with an occasional song from the colorful *Hymns Hot and Carols Cool* or one of its successors, which at these times appear in the pews along with the traditional book.

As we stand to sing our praise or penitence, we are surrounded by reminders that our faith is alive in a continuing fellowship. Between the stained-glass windows with their ancient meaningful symbols hangs a series of colorful modern banners made by our women. Each represents one of the historic confessions of faith, from the Nicene Creed down to the United Presbyterian Confession of 1967, and on those special days when we sing "The Great Parade" with its rousing tune, we know ourselves to be part of the worldwide family of God: "people of all times and places, people of all nations and races," "young people, old people, quiet people, bold people." We may even march around inside the church to the beat of a drum and other Orff instruments played by a group of children and young people who have been dubbed "the Orffans." We are a "singing, swinging procession and here am I, here am I!" [1] Gloria in excelsis Deo!

Children not only enjoy variety in rhythm, they want to learn how to keep time to it, whether they begin by rocking back and forth, or clapping hands, or stamping their feet. In preschool groups, rhythm sticks can help give them a good start. They are easy to use and inexpensive.

At first, children need a lead from the teacher at the piano or with her own singing voice as they try to hit the sticks together on the first beat of each measure. Then as they grow more sure of their timing—for that they need an opportunity to grope around and fail a bit—they can begin to fill in the unaccented notes too. It's fun to listen carefully so you can come down ZING! on that first beat every time. It's fun to improve until you can add all the patter to fit the music in between.

In July 1970 the Choristers Guild held a seminar in Wichita, Kansas, during which Helen Kemp led a Primary Choir demonstration. In an account of her purposes and procedures in the Choristers Guild Letter for September,

[1] *The Great Parade.* © 1971, Richard K. Avery and Donald S. Marsh. Used by permission.

1970, she speaks of the need that children have for success in musical learning and how she tries to pass on to them what she calls "seedling" skills. To help them understand what makes a song, she uses a teaching chant:

> A song has a pulse, has a pulse, has a pulse,
> A song has a beat like your heart—
> Steady, steady, feel it flow
> Sometimes fast, sometimes slow.
>
> A song has a rhythm of the words, of the words,
> A song has a *rise* and a *Fall*
> Words have syl-la-bles, STRONG and weak
> Some we ac-cent, some not at all.
>
> A song has a line, has a line, has a line
> A line that pulls through the beat
> Spins through the rhythm of the word, of the words
> To make each thought complete
>
> A song has a spirit, and a lift, and a lilt,
> A song gives wings to words
> A song can sigh, or fly up high!
> A song is for us ALL, not just the BIRDS! [2]

In the Choristers Guild Letter for October 1970, there is a fascinating account of how the rhythm in the Hawaiian carol "Al-le-lu!" was introduced at a demonstration workshop in Hawaii. First the entire group was led in a few basic Hula movements with their characteristic flowing style. Even the drumbeat was relaxed instead of angular and hard. Next, the entire carol was interpreted in dance, using an easygoing tempo. The account goes on to say that the opening chant was conversational rather than dramatic,

---

[2] Choristers Guild Letters.

a sensitive way to evaluate the mood of a piece of music.

To help children of Junior age appreciate the metrics of traditional hymns, the teacher can call attention to the series of numerals printed at the top of the page in most hymnals, which indicate the number of syllables in each line of the words, and then lead them in clapping rhythm together. Or she may clap the rhythm of another familiar hymn alone and let them guess which one it is. As children become more skilled, they too can take turns clapping the rhythm while the others guess. This is a game that requires both familiarity with hymn tunes and precision in listening, for some of the meters closely resemble each other. For example, Beethoven's "Hymn to Joy," which provides the music for "Joyful, Joyful, We Adore Thee," is in the metre 8.7.8.7, while Salzburg ("Let the Whole Creation Cry") is 7.7.7.7, a pleasant variety. It would make an interesting experiment to compare the meters of the classic tunes with the contemporary and experience the difference without even singing the melody the first time. For example, "Take Time," the new Epiphany carol mentioned earlier, is 8.6.8.6.8.5.8.4. In this way children might begin to develop appreciation for the art of the composer in different periods or styles. They can see that rhythm is related to structure, which makes music a kind of cousin to architecture, an exciting discovery.

Less academic are the singing games that are a delight because they add a spirit of play to the singing and the movement. The photograph opposite shows Eva Rozgonyi of Budapest leading children in a singing game at the Kodály workshop at the 1973 summer school at Chautauqua, New York.

Children sitting around a table like to put their hands out in front of them, palms down, and beat out different rhythms as a group, the teacher leading at first to keep them together. Some like to mark the time alone as a "solo" and others like to try leading the group themselves. This can be done as an accompaniment to a piano, or their own singing, or recorded music. This is also useful in leadership-training sessions for teachers.

In our youth choirs an alert sense of rhythm comes less from drill than from an inner freedom to feel and to express that feeling. If the music is lively, the members may snap their fingers spontaneously or, if they happen to be standing, even dance a few steps now and then, If the director calls for volunteers to conduct a song, usually all hands go up. He gives each one the opportunity to try a simple arm movement alone with the piano before

the voices come in. It is an exciting moment, especially if it is the first time . . . an adventure of leadership. For those in the field of rhythm who continue their interest, there may even be an opportunity to conduct during a Sunday morning service of worship. Then everyone is proud and happy: children, parents, the entire gathered family.

There seems to be no evidence that Jesus ever sang with the children who came to him. Most of the music Jewish children might have heard in Palestine at that time would have been related to the singing of psalms in the Temple, laments for the dead, or the celebration of a wedding feast. There may have been some Greek influence in secular music in Jerusalem for a time, but Jewish authorities were alert to the danger of diluting their tradition by too easy an assimilation with alien cultures. The great rise of folksongs among the dispersed Jews in Europe came centuries later.

But it is hard to imagine Jesus and the fishermen sailing out across the Sea of Galilee without singing. You would think the wind and sun and spray would have turned them on. We know that Jesus told stories that made people listen whether they were rebuked or comforted or aroused. What would he have sung had he had a guitar? What would he have sung to the children?

In our church we have a copy of a painting by Richard Hook, showing children gathered about Jesus as though they might have been singing together a few moments before. Jesus is smiling and the children look alive and completely at home with their leader, themselves, and each other. Music, like love, draws people together and puts a sparkle in their eyes.

I have seen children of the choir, grumpy and out of sorts after a long day at school, begin to relax and smile when Don Marsh goes to the piano for a few rousing chords and leads them in a song. They are alive again and ready for an hour and a half of learning and fellowship that will pass all too quickly.

The nurturing for this fellowship became apparent one day when I was helping with the children after their rehearsal. The copy of Hook's painting was on an easel near one end of the table where everyone was gathering for a "business meeting." Don Marsh was sitting at the other end when the choir president called for the minutes. Some of the younger children were grouped around his chair as close as they could get. Suddenly Bonna, who was next to me, sat up straight, looking intently at Don and the group around him.

"Look," she whispered in my ear, "they're the same!" And she motioned from the group to the picture on the easel.

I saw what she meant and nodded.

"Shall we tell them?" she asked.

We looked at each other and back at the group and decided not to. It might make them self-conscious if we told how we knew that the Jesus kind of love was right here in our own choir. Bonna had seen it and shared with me. It made us both happy in a special kind of way.

One year, children in our parish were introduced to their teachers and each other in a memorable way—through rhythm. On a large bulletin board the outline of a tree with spreading branches represented the church family, and as each child arrived he was given a bright-colored paper leaf to write his name on. The children went to the board one at a time while Don improvised on the piano to suit the walk of each. Because he knows the children so well, each bit of music was like an artist's drawing. Then, when each child had pinned his name firmly on the tree he turned and said: "My name is ——." The entire group repeated the name together four times after which Steve Carlton, one of the "Orffans," produced a short flourish on the metalaphone in a rhythm that matched the syllables of the name:

    Jen-i-fer   (3 notes)
    Brad-ley   (2 notes)
    Bob   (only 1 note, but good and strong)

It would not surprise me to learn that each child that day had been introduced not only to his teachers and class-mates but also to himself.

2

Relationship, Worship,
and Music

T H R O U G H the centuries music has been associated
with worship in the Church. The people of Israel sang to
the Lord when they were brought safely through the Red
Sea . . . "for he hath triumphed gloriously . . ." and Miriam
led the women as they danced and sang to His glory
with their tambourines. Music is mentioned throughout
the Old Testament and must have been quite thoroughly
established as a part of Hebrew culture in general. In
Genesis it is referred to along with the forging of iron
tools as though both were equally a part of daily life,
so that it would be quite natural for the people to sing
and play instruments in relating themselves to God. Samuel,
the last of the judges, even founded a school for the training of musicians to serve in the Temple where both choirs
and an orchestra led the congregation in antiphonal
singing.

We can only guess what the music itself was like because
we have no record of the musical notation of that day,
but we do know that the people who climbed the hill to
worship in Jerusalem were singing or chanting psalms.

What a sight, what a sound, the procession of men, women, and children in their long, bright robes swinging their way up the slopes of Mount Moriah to the Temple, listening to the song of the choirs within, and giving their own exultant response as they ascend the steps to the inner courts of worship. Now they hear the lyre and the flute and timbrel and catch the scent of the smoke of sacrifice as they recall their past and hope for the future, praising God for His mighty saving power:

> Fling wide the gates,
>> open the ancient doors,
>> and the great king will come in.
> Who is this great king?
> He is the Lord, strong and mighty,
>> the Lord, victorious in battle!
>>> from Psalm 24:7-8
>>> Today's English Version

No ordinary building, this. In Hebrew it is sometimes referred to as the "Palace of Jehovah," and to honor the one God, David planned that it would be His very house, taking care to provide for it costly furnishings, rare and precious ornaments.

All this grandeur and beauty was destroyed when the king of Babylon captured Jerusalem and took the people away captive. Some fifty years or so later Nehemiah rebuilt it, twice the size of the first Temple but not nearly so beautiful. It was at this second Temple that the book of Psalms became the official hymnbook of the Hebrew faith, the same one from which Jesus would sing five hundred years later as both child and man in the local synagogue at Nazareth, and on his memorable visit to the Temple at the age of twelve. He would hear there the trained choirs for the first time and respond with his parents from that official hymnbook. Again, it would be a hymn from the same collection that Jesus would sing with his disciples at their last meal together before he went to his betrayal and death, and still later it was the first hymnbook of the early Christian Church.

In their secret gatherings in private homes or at the place of family burial beneath the streets of Rome, Christians would have to be more restrained in their song than the exultant worshipers in the Temple, for fear of being discovered by the Roman guards. As it had been with Moses during the hard times in Egypt, so it was with the early Christians. They often had to hide to survive.

In spite of storm and stress in the life of the Church, music has with few exceptions persisted as the companion of worship in Christian celebration. One wonders why. Even in the bleak days of religious conflict in Scotland when no organ was permitted in the service, the psalms could still be intoned by the minister and responded to by the congregation. Perhaps the simple answer is that music is so basic to our welfare, it is too good to miss. If Plato was right when he said, "Music and rhythm find their way into the secret places of the soul," then even if we try, we shall not be able to discard it permanently.

Worship means different things to different people: wonder, communion, commitment, renewal, joy, a sense of being alive, a sense of direction, compassion. The late Dr. John Bruére says in *Religion That Works* that the word "worship" itself is the key to its meaning: "ascribe value to." What do we value most? What comes first in our lives? That is what we worship. All men worship something. Not all men worship God.

How do we come to it? No creative activity can be contained in a rigid formula. Yet some of the elements of the worship experience may be more dependable than others, and among these at the top of the list I would place the arts. This does not mean that feeling is "all." Music, painting, drama express ideas and convictions as well as emotion and each has to produce something that can be seen or heard in order to exist. I agree with Martin Luther, whose enthusiasm for singing did not prevent his insistence on the objective support of both the written and the spoken word—the Bible and the sermon. "A Mighty Fortress Is Our God" is a teaching hymn, almost a sermon in itself.

Few churches today would be content to choose music for a worship service as though it were an afterthought or a gimmick to fill up time. The intent, rather, is to weave it into the other elements of the worship like one of the colorful threads of a tapestry.

I recall a memorable account of a worship service planned in just that way for an ecumenical group which included boys and girls from three major Protestant denominations as well as the Roman Catholic and Eastern Orthodox.[1] The theme for the day had been related to "communion" and called for both discussion and celebration of its meaning. Because so many traditions were represented, the leaders realized they were being challenged to give the children an experience that would help them to understand that the sacrament is not confined to one single event of taking bread and wine together at church, but that Christians of any age can have communion with each other in many different ways.

The group sat in a circle out doors on the ground and, after talking together about the meaning of the African folksong "Kum Ba Yah," sang it as their call to worship. Then the hymn "For the Beauty of the Earth" was sung by the teacher and children responsively. Singing it outdoors made it a special song of praise. The Scripture which

[1] By Margaret Adams, educational consultant to the Presbytery of Baltimore. Used by permission.

followed was from the Phillips translation of Ephesians
3:14:

> And I pray that you . . . may be able to grasp (with all
> Christians) how wide and deep and long and high is the
> love of Christ—and to know for yourselves that love so
> far beyond our comprehension.

Now the group was ready to try associating other words
that relate in some way to "communion": community,
communal, communicate, common, etc. Some of the comments showed unexpected insight: communal—everyone
using the same thing, like rest rooms out in public, or the
farms in Russia; common—being alike, having something
that brings things or persons together (like color, shape,
interest).

From there the group went on to talk about meanings
of communion other than the special ritual at church:
forgiveness, love, being close to each other, trying to
understand each other. The children gave revealing ex-
amples of such kinds of communion: "when my mom fed
a 'bum' lunch in our kitchen and she let me talk to him";
"when the doctor told my sister that her new baby would
live"; "when the gang decided not to tease Jimmy about
his dad having to go to jail"; etc. "When our church
had its Strawberry Festival and everyone had such a good
time together they didn't want to go home." When the
children were asked why they thought communion was
important they mentioned the need to forgive each other;
the fun of being with friends; the command of Jesus to
love everyone, even people we think we can't like; and
because he said this is one way to remember him.

To illustrate how we can show each other that we care,
the teacher invited them to share a large red apple with
her. She said it could represent the prayer they would
all like to pray with Paul in the church at Ephesus: "that

they [and we] might grasp with all Christians how wide
and deep and long and high is the love of Christ." They
talked about what the different parts of the apple could
mean: the skin holds everything together . . . it's like
what makes us common. The red color is like red blood.
The core is where the seeds are, protected by it. Like God
protecting us, always ready to forgive and love us. After
a prayer thanking God for the gifts of communion and
asking that each be more open to the opportunities for
communion all around, they passed the kiss of peace and
found that no one wanted to leave. They felt a strange
new bond that made them one. "Someone's singing, Lord,
Kum Ba Yah!"

There was a time when the leaders of vacation church
schools and winter Sunday schools led opening and closing
"exercises" instead of worship. Songs were chosen for their
rousing fervor rather than their meaning. Sometimes the
children would be asked to call out their favorites, and
one may suppose that "Stand Up, Stand Up for Jesus"
was one of the top ten, for what child could fail to be
stirred by these battle cries: "lift high the royal banner,"
"the trumpet call obey," "forth to the mighty conflict
against unnumbered foes," "let courage rise with danger
and strength to strength oppose!" But there were no actual
banners and seldom if ever a trumpet, and no hint as to
what the danger was or who the foes. Without a story,
a discussion, or a symbol to point up the purpose of all
that zeal and move the children toward some common goal,
the end result must have been an emotional binge rather
than an act of worship. The new *Worshipbook* of the
Presbyterian Church has omitted this song, perhaps for the
reason I have suggested, perhaps because the vocabulary
is obsolete. Both are valid reasons, yet I confess to a certain
nostalgia when I found it was missing from the index, for

although I attended a church of a different denomination, we did sing that song and it was the only thing I recall being moved by on a Sunday morning except the minister's kind face. I wish we could have been guided like that ecumenical group just described. Instead of the sense of unity and joy they experienced as they passed the Peace, we listened to the superintendent's statistical report given faithfully every week as the climax of the day: number present today, number present a week ago today, number present a year ago today . . . and how much the Collection was on each of those occasions.

There have been many changes since that time, with new curricula and materials, new emphasis on social responsibility, which long since have made that kind of Sunday school a travesty. Today there is a further ferment in values, stirring us to think of new ways in both music and worship. A Lutheran minister writes a book called the *Worship Workbench*, a young priest binds his stories of celebration together with the title *Wonder and Worship*, a minister and choir director issue an informal monthly newsletter "in the Worship Workshop with Avery and Marsh," national committees meet to share ideas, sift the wheat from the chaff, and inspire new growth. In Berkeley, California, John and Mary Harrell create and publish new forms for worship that a variety of ages can enjoy. Thousands of people travel a distance to participate in workshops for creative worship.

A new venture for publishing contemporary church music springs up surprisingly in what was once a funeral parlor, and the "Proclamation Productions" of Port Jervis becomes a living symbol of both resurrection and creation. At the door of the remodeled house are a banner and a trumpet, and the songs they proclaim are relevant! Established firms such as the Hope Publishing Company and Agape are issuing colorful new editions with creative ideas and singable tunes, and many of the major denominations have brought out revised hymnbooks, some of which contain at least a few contemporary composers. The indexes are carefully organized to show the bearing each hymn has on the life of people and the life of the church as an institution, on the celebration of the Christian Year, and events in civic life of significance for the nation or the world. At least one volume includes a section on ecology. Lay leaders will find this helpful in choosing songs relevant to the lives of those who sing them.

In Canada, the Anglican and United churches have joined in a common venture to produce *The Hymnbook* authorized by both bodies in 1971. During the 1960s the Scottish church set up a series of experimental consultations at Dunblane which led to publishing contemporary material, beginning with *Dunblane Praises* I and II, and progressed to others published by Galliard in England: *Songs for the Seventies, New Life* (for teenagers), *New Orbit* (for under-elevens). Then there is the "Faith, Folk and ———" series (Clarity, Festivity, Nativity, etc.) edited by Peter Smith, who is vitally interested in contemporary forms of Christian expression, especially those using the idiom of folk music. In the United States, there are now six books in the series that began with *Hymns Hot and Carols Cool*, each bound in a different color of the rainbow. Two collections of songs for children are of special interest: *Sing for Joy* (Seabury Press) beamed to those of three to eight years, and *Sing of Life and Faith* (Pilgrim Press) for the first six grades.

In *Sing for Joy* there are four main sections relating children through song to the Christian Year and the Church, to praising God and giving thanks, to the wonders of creation, and to His loving care for all people. The songs are alive, where the children are, as titles indicate: "Mitten Song," "Morning at the Beach," "Come to My

House." In the unit on Heaven and Earth, look for "The Woodpecker" among the songs on "Birds, Bugs, and Beasts." You will feel the urge to look up a pair of rhythm sticks and try out the song yourself, if you don't already know it, and then give it to your group.

Don't miss the song "Jesus Is Coming," with a tune from a Welsh carol, or "The Sunday Bells Are Ringing" with directions for simple movements. The rhythm is vigorous and the words convey a sense of joyous fellowship:

> The Sunday bells are ringing
> A ding a ding a ding;
>
> Come all good Christian people
> O come to Church and sing.
> Come fathers all and mothers,
> Come sisters and come brothers.
>
> The Sunday bells are ringing,
> A ding a ding a ding.[2]

Toward the end of the book are the songs for work as well as play. "I Can Help" (pick up toys, wipe the spoons, sing a song) has possible variations like "Will you help?" "John can help," "Who will help?" The song "Cooperation" is a good one if the mother is at home and only Daddy works. For the "liberated" household, new words are in order. "We're Making Valentines," "Fingerpainting," and a "Put Away Song" can help move things along happily. For fun there is "The Train" with exciting sounds to make, and "Here's the Bus" that is good for dramatic play. "Jim Along Josie" has rhythmic activity galore from running, skipping, walking, and stretching to crawling. When you are ready to absorb more, turn to page 128 and

[2] In *Sing for Joy*, Norman and Margaret Mealy, eds. (New York: Seabury Press, 1961).

read the helpful articles on "The Use of Music with Young Children" by Norman and Margaret Mealy, compilers of the book.

Sing of Life and Faith is the United Church of Christ hymnbook for children of Primary and Junior age. It is the only hymnal for children as far as I know in which the songs are all directly related to the theological stand of the church (in this instance, to the main divisions of the Statement of Faith adopted by the United Church in 1959).

The committee and the editors have paid special attention not only to the literary and educational value of the material, but also to the biblical and theological soundness of the texts. Both traditional and contemporary material is included. "We Shall Overcome" is only three pages away from "The God of Abraham Praise" with its traditional Hebrew melody from about 1400. "If I Had a Hammer" is not far from Frances Havergal's "Take My Life and Let It Be" of the nineteenth century, with a tune harmonized by J. S. Bach over a hundred years earlier. There is a wide variety of folktune sources, including the Bohemian Brethren, Latvia, Denmark, Wales, Silesia, the West Indies, and America's own Southern Harmony and New England.

Jacob Trapp wrote the words in 1932 for a song of hope, "Wonders Still the World Shall Witness"; Jeannette Perkins Brown the words for "We Thank You God for Eyes to See," using a traditional English melody. Our youth choirs often sing "Thank You" by Martin G. Schneider, both words and music written in 1962. The West Indian setting for the Lord's Prayer circled the globe (including Port Jervis) during a recent World Day of Prayer. But I have told enough. Each collection of songs has treasure to be discovered and it is not fair to spoil the fun of hunting.

When conditions permit, healthy children often have a

quick perception of how things are which I like to call "instant access." They come into the true presence of people or dogs, trees or flowers or running brooks without distortion or fear. One day while walking with my neighbor of five to the grocery store on the corner, she treated me to this experience: as we were passing a house set in a large lawn, she halted abruptly and pointed. "Look!" "Look!" I looked and saw what I would have missed, a single yellow rose on a single slender bush in the center of the lawn. She ran across the grass and I followed. Laughing and clapping her hands with delight, she bent down and smelled the flower. So did I. That was when we both discovered the tiny wire fence around the rose. Protecting it, caring. Neither of us said a word. We just slapped our knees and rocked with laughter at the loveable absurdity of it all. Now when our minister Richard Avery reminds the congregation that God loves each one of us as though we were the only person in the world, and yet loves everyone in that same extravagant way, I remember the yellow rose.

> Why do I
> see more
> going to the store
> with a child?
>
> Because she
> helps me to be
> as a child,
> that's why!

Such experiences were not rare but regular in the life of the man of Assisi. He seemed able to maintain a consistently childlike spirit, and it has been a pleasant discovery for me to learn only recently that singing helped him do it. He spent much time, he says, "singing forth with a low

voice my contemplations of the Creator and Redeemer.
. . . It always seemed natural to me to sing or chant forth
my meditations."

In the summer of 1970 some of us opened an experimental class in the dining room of our church where children could experience many things, both indoors and out,
under the shade tree at the back, or in the park across the
way. It was to be a Vacation School with a difference:
children under twelve in our own church and community
in a fresh experience of relationship. We decided not to
have rigid age groups, but to begin all together and have
an adjoining room set up for those who might indicate
as the morning progressed that they needed building
blocks or a housekeeping center or a different pace. We
used no official curriculm but developed our own to give
maximum opportunity for a growing experience for each
child.

Our theme was "The Expanding Circle, Beginning with
Me," and in this frame of reference we hoped each child
would enjoy being alive and discovering more of his own
identity, the joy of common things, of making friends, and
becoming more aware of the community. We knew that
"making friends" would be a process and we could not
predict how far it would move from mere acceptance of
each other but we hoped it would go at least as far as
knowing each other better, then on to liking and enjoying.
We wanted to provide opportunities for doing all kinds of
things such as singing, dancing, drawing, playing games,
listening to stories and talking about them, wishing, col-
lecting nature things, "tripping," helping, celebrating, and
worshiping. We planned not to begin with God (although
everything does!) but hopefully praying to move toward
Him in awareness as far as we could. Although we consciously guided some of the activity, we kept it free-flow-
ing from day to day, allowing for choices and surprise. I

think the leaders all believed that God is real and available to give a nudge now and then if plans might have to be amended, but we did not go into the matter specifically and might have been enriched by it if we had. Perhaps things would have gone even better. Perhaps there were times when we did operate as though God were on some distant planet instead of in the room with all of us.

Because we planned our activities in terms of what we hoped they might do for the children, a scenario of the beginning of the first day is included below. The happenings are factual, "How I Feel" represents what we hoped in advance might happen for the "average" child who would engage in those activities.

Here I Am: Me	*What's Happening*	*How I Feel*
I have a name.	At the door a teacher smiles and says, "Come in." She gives me a name tag. I print my name. She helps me pin it on. *Her* name is "Aunt Sue."	They *want* me here.
I am growing but don't know how tall I am.	Donith measures me with a yardstick. 44 inches.	44 inches! I like knowing.
I like colors. I like to choose. I can draw.	Aunt Kay says I can make a sign with my inches on it. She shows me the table with colored paper and crayons.	I go and start one. I am having fun.
I am not alone.	Other children are drawing too.	It's fun to make things together.
Mine's done.	Nancy is putting chairs in a circle, I go over and help. Other children come and help too.	Everybody is helping together.
We are sitting in a circle.	We hold our signs. We tell our names and show our signs.	I am Somebody, and I am learning other kids' names and things.

Aunt Dorothy tells us we
can hang our signs up
anywhere. We get some
sticking stuff and run
around to find a good
place.

I like to be busy.
I like to decide
things.

Jane hangs hers on a
window. Bill puts his on
a door. The girl with a
Band-aid is putting hers
on the board. She's 45
inches. I hang mine up
high on a wall. I have to
reach. I'm 44 inches.

Our signs are all
around. Some-
thing is happen-
ing. We did it.
We are impor-
tant!

I like to try
hard things.

We had chosen three special songs for the backbone of our
plan, and only the third was from a hymnbook. We were
ready for the first right now, old enough to be new to
the children and familiar to most of the teachers, a song
from "The King and I":[3]

Getting to know you
Getting to know all about you
Getting to like you
Getting to hope you'll like me.

Instead of using the piano, we put on a record so that we
could all get into the act. Everyone perked up and went
into a circle, catching the beat, skipping, listening to the
words, reversing the circle, beginning to sing. It was an

[3] "Getting to Know You" from *The King and I*. Music by Richard
Rodgers. Lyrics by Oscar Hammerstein II. © Copyright 1951 by
Richard Rodgers and Oscar Hammerstein II, Williamson Music, Inc.,
445 Park Avenue, New York, N.Y. 10022, owner of publication and
allied rights for all countries of Western Hemisphere. Used by permission. All Rights Reserved.

instant hit with everyone. If "You are precisely my cup of
tea" was Greek to some, they knew "free and easy" and
came in with flying colors on the finale:

Haven't you noticed?
Suddently I'm bright and breezy
Because of
All the beautiful and new
Things I'm learning about you,
Day by day.

The second or third time through the older children
wanted to circle in the "grand chain," manner of the
square dance, but that was too much for the youngest.
They dropped out and went into the next room with
Donith, a teenage helper, where they played until it was
time to go outdoors. The fact that we could not all finish
the morning together did not spoil the fun of being together for the beginning of it.

Every day we did familiar things for stability, and new
things for growing. We always had singing, a circle for
out-loud reading, and a book table for browsing. We had
games outdoors, a juice break, and a chance to make something. And every morning we brought our nature finds to
the treasure table as soon as we arrived. Common things
around us that turn uncommon when you see how beautiful they really are. Birch bark with dual personality, one
outside, another inside. Pebbles and stones to hold in the
hand for rough or smooth and no two quite the same in
color. Ferns and flowers and grainlike grasses to put in
jars of water for caring, green velvet moss to lay on
colored paper. Apricot? yellow? madonna blue? Shells big
and little and, if lucky, one that gives your hard-pressed
ear the distant murmur of an imagined ocean. Patterns too,
in leaves from maple, oak, or tulip tree, from clover and

the dandelion. And the twigs. The sturdy unpredictable twigs, sharp and provocative like a protest. The bringing and the arranging of these treasures and the sharing became an informal ritual and kept eyes sharp to look and see between our times together. We were getting ourselves ready for the third song that would support our class experience, the third "spine song": "Lord God from Whom All Life."

But I have not yet mentioned the second spine song, "It's a Small World," from the Walt Disney film. This is the song we choreographed on the day the children drew their own eyes, trying to make the color unmistakably their own. As we continued to try for self-respect and confidence in a variety of ways, we also tried to move out from self toward others. So after putting up their drawings, we chose partners for a dance, shook hands, spoke each other's names (noting the color of our partner's eyes), and moved in a simple pattern like a reel until everyone had danced with everybody else. Each time through, the children were more familiar with the words until they could do words and movement at the same time, "free and easy." At that point we really came together in song and dance.

    It's a world of laughter, a world of tears;
    it's a world of hopes and a world of fears.
    There's so much that we share
    that it's time we're aware,
    It's a small world after all.

    Chorus: It's a small world after all
            It's a small world after all,
            It's a small world after all
            It's a small, small world.

There is just one moon and one golden sun
and a smile means friendship for ev'ry one.
Though the mountains divide
and the oceans are wide,
It's a small world after all.[4]

Every day the children wanted to dance the world small, and repeat the "Getting to Know You" song and routine. They liked fun songs too, but the others seemed to be their favorites. It was about this time we made a chart for the easel to remind ourselves that knowing people is not all candy. Here is a rough idea of the chart:

Most of our days were glad days but we were troubled about Tracy. On the opening day when we gave him his

---

[4] "It's a Small World." Words and Music by Richard M. and Robert B. Sherman. © 1936 Wonderland Music Company, Inc. Used by permission.

name tag he had seemed embarrassed and did not want to
wear it, and on the day the children drew their self-por-
traits, he finished his but suddenly took a black crayon
and made a large X across the face from corner to corner.
We had hung our favorite picture of Jesus and the children
on the bulletin board and now invited the class to put their
own portraits around it. Tracy put his up with the others
and there it was, next to Miriam's and Debbie's and Jeff's,
scar and all.

Instead of going to the circle for the story that day we
sat on the floor around the pictures and I told the story of
Jesus and the children based on the tenth chapter of Mark.
Tracy gave complete attention and joined thoughtfully in
singing "Jesus loves the little children—they are precious in
his sight." If we had known Mr. Rogers's song at the time,
we would have sung that too: "Everybody's Fancy."

When we decided to make a sign, "Let the Children
Come," to pin up near Jesus and another with just the one
word "Me" to go with their own group of portraits, Tracy
seemed glad to help. Was a little warmth getting through?

The stories and poems for reading aloud were carefully
chosen. "Horton Hears a Hoo" by Dr. Seuss was a favorite
not only for the illustrations but also for his main point,
which the children had no difficulty making their own: a
person is a person no matter how small. They liked the
poem "Hands" by Dorothy Aldis, and "Feet" by the same
writer. Later they traced their own hands and feet on
heavy paper of different colors and cut them out. Like
people, they were the same yet different, and all traveling
on the same boat, so to speak. Why not make a mobile of
all hands on board to swing from the light fixture in the
ceiling?

So we did, and the next day another one of all the feet.
When the two mobiles were both moving airily overhead,
it was fun to pick out your own up there, taking the breeze

with all the others. Once again, a self-awareness and moving out—this time *up*, and doing it with friends.

From making his own portrait with crayons, each child went on to make one of his family from bits of colored paper torn to represent them—the "torn-paper medium"! This proved to be an absorbing activity for the children and a revealing one to us. Depending on the maturity or happiness of each child, members of the family came out as mere strips of paper, straight and stiff, or well-proportioned figures skillfully rounded out. One child chose a neutral tan background for his family on which he pasted both parents and children torn from the same colorless paper. As a result the entire family was indistinct, the parents and children indistinguishable from each other. Another child let the children stand out in contrasting color, important and distinct, but melted his parents into the background.

With so far to go, shall we really overcome? Not unless, like the donkey in the Christmas song, we "move on! move on! Little donkey, move on!"

We did move on, outwardly at least, into the community to play games in the park and take walks in the neighborhood, and also for special trips. One day we went to the public library to see a children's film on poetry. We had frolicked through a lot of poems and hoped that when we came back from the library there would be some inspired verse-writing among us, but we had not yet felt enough together for poetry to come naturally. Maybe it was the July heat, maybe the film was too intellectual, maybe we pushed for too much too soon. Whatever it was, in contrast, the Humane Society Animal Shelter really turned them on. Back at the church after the trip there was a burst of creative activity. Remembering the homeless dogs and cats they had seen in cages, the warm puppies they had cuddled, and the bright-eyed kittens, they reached for

clay, with their hearts in their hands, and fell to modeling
in a kind of ecstasy. It was time to start learning the song
of praise in earnest:

> Lord God from whom all life
> And all true gladness springs
> Whose love and care
> Shine everywhere
> Among earth's common things.[5]

We were getting close to a much wider circle.

We came closer again the day we experienced the difference between a wish and a prayer. We had been reading poems on wishing . . . for courage to do the right even
if laughed at . . . for better manners . . . and to remember
to feed the dog. Several times we had wished the best thing
we could think of for the person on each side of us in the
circle, silently, turning to the left and then to the right so
that each person knew who was wishing for him as well as
the one he was wishing for. There was a sense of unity and
communion at these times, preparation for the day when
we would verbally include God and the wish would be a
prayer. That turned out to be a very special day because
our minister, Richard Avery, popped in as a surprise and
joined the circle. We had a prayer of thanks together and
the circle went "Zoom a-Zoom!"

Like life itself, our experimental class had its ups and
downs, and not all of the downs could be laid at the door
of Tracy. In fact, the scene of the most harrowing episode
we had was the cellar door at the back of the church, and
Tracy was not remotely involved. Three of the boys were
romping there during outdoor play and when I left the

[5] "Lord God from Whom All Life," words by the late Bishop E. A.
Burroughs from *Songs of Praise*, enlarged edition, published in 1931 by
Oxford University Press, London, Used by permission of the SPCK,
London.

yard to go inside, they were using the door as a slide, taking turns in the accepted playground manner. But moments later, something went wrong with the vibrations. Peace was shattered by sounds of torment from the area of the cellar door. Several of us arrived at the scene in time to see the smallest of the three boys go down under the attack of the other two who gleefully pinned him to the ground as he struggled unsuccessfully to get free. Two against one. A demonic moment. What we did immediately to impose a cease-fire was important, but not so significant as the talk we had together in a quiet room inside. I don't remember all that was said, but everyone spoke out and there was a coming together in understanding and forgiveness.

Compared with Tracy's difficulties, which enlisted compassion, this experience was horrifying, irrational. Cruelty has a sinister element lacking in the troubles of Tracy. It is as though the warmth of Jesus' life might help Tracy, but only the surgery of his death could heal the behavior at the cellar door.

We could be much more innovative in our work with children in this dimension, the need for forgiveness or even just their need to say, "I'm sorry." We can help them recognize the difference between making a mistake in carelessness and hurting someone on purpose. The following letter came to me from an adult helper in a craft class that met on Fridays in New York. She was from Japan and spoke broken English, but took the trouble to say she was sorry in writing. It could not have been easy but she did it:

> Dear Mrs. Wright:
> I must beg you and all my wood-cut class children and others. In this morning I have been great mistake that felt like Saturday. When I noticed my mistake, it was too late. I could not make contact to you.

What shall I do!
Now I am shaming myself deeply profoundly for
my own carelessness and unscrupulousness.
                              Sincerely yours,
                              Hanaogi

Although that letter represents a mistake rather than a
sin, I wish I had thought of reading it to the children in
connection with the boys' fight, and singing the "sorry"
song after we had the sharing time.

> For the things that I've done wrong
> Things that I remember long,
> Hurting friends and those I love
> I am very sorry, God.[6]

Songs like this can be a release for an entire group.
Another song, "We want to learn to live in love," by M.
Dosia Carlson, could be helpful. Here is the third stanza:

> When others are unkind to us
> and make us want to cry or fight,
> We can reach out to be good friends,
> And help them know that love is right.[7]

It is a song of discipleship written for children, but how
nice if we *all* took it seriously! For a while I wondered if
a song from Yugoslavia in the UNICEF *Book of Songs for
Children* might be useful in this effort. It is a dialogue
between a child and a butterfly who suspects that the child's
friendly advances are only a ruse to get near enough to
capture him and stick him with a needle. The butterfly
escapes unharmed, but we are left with the conviction that
the butterfly was right and the child did intend to torture

---

[6] In *Sing for Joy* (New York: Seabury Press, 1961).
[7] In *Sing of Life and Faith* (Philadelphia: Pilgrim Press, 1969).

him if not actually kill him. On further thought, I would not recommend the song for all young children. There might be a rash of raids on butterflies. Better a round from the same book, "How Good and Joyous for Brothers to Dwell Together."

Before the birthday celebration for those born during the summer, we carefully practiced "Lord God from Whom All Life" to give the song a fair chance. Some of the phrases were out of date here and there so we put those in today's English to make the meaning clear. We could have chosen a contemporary song in the first place, but the lilting tune was too good to miss, and anyway knowing music from different periods makes for variety.

We said Grace before we cut the cake: "Thank you for giving us life," and someone piped up "It's the best birthday gift there is." Then we sang our song:

> Lord God from whom all life
> and all true gladness springs. . . .

If I were doing this again, I would choose a contemporary song to go with this, possibly Fred Rogers's "It's Such a Good Feeling" (to know you're alive). Since it is written for younger children, the two songs together would help handle age differences.

The next day we sang all of our special songs, and the thank-you prayer was a big one. For one thing, someone had forgotten to bring a key we needed that day and Donith had volunteered to walk some distance to get it. When we went into the circle later, we talked about God helping people and whose hands and feet he uses. We were sitting under the mobiles we had made, our hands and feet, and someone said: "Donith. She got the key with *her* hands and feet." So Donith had been helping God to help us.

The story for that day had been "Brenda Brave Helps

Grandmother," and we talked a good bit about kindness.
Everything was adding up. When we bowed our heads
and everyone had a chance to say what he was thankful
for, there were not long pauses: "Thank you for hands and
feet." "Thank you for Donith." "Thank you for the
people who gave the shelter for homeless pets." "Thank
you for the birthday party and the cake." "Thank you for
Kool-Aid." Then unexpectedly someone said, "Dear God,
you love us all if we're short or if we're tall." At last a
poem! Then Bill, a thoughtful boy who usually said little,
raised his head and looked directly at us teachers: "Thank
you to the teachers for teaching me."

Our hearts were full. We had been getting to know-
like-enjoy each other. Now we were getting to love each
other. We were in the widest circle. What are the words
in Whittier's hymn? "To worship rightly is to love each
other."

The next day was Thursday, our last day together, and
we thought it would be an anticlimax after the happenings
on Wednesday, but love has its surprises. This time there
were two.

Just before closing time we went for a walk in the
neighborhood, admiring the flowers in the gardens we
passed. At one home they were so beautiful we trespassed
for a closer look, not to pick, only to smell. But the lady
(?) of the house rushed out and startled the children with
her accusations. We tried to explain but could not be sure
she understood. Too many people think that approaching
a flower means you want to possess it. The second surprise
was a plus instead of a minus. Turning the next corner, we
beheld a giant chestnut tree in bloom. "Beheld" is the only
word for it.

"Let's make a wish," cried someone, and we stopped
talking and looked up into the branches through white
blossoms, waiting for the right thought to form. Suddenly

it happened, but not what we had expected. Not a wish at all, more like the fulfillment of a wish. Like the Parousia! Halfway up the tree there was a rapid shaking of the leaves and flowers and a dazzling flash of fur as a squirrel leapt out of hiding and slid along a large limb for one brief instant before he disappeared. We saw it together in awe, with a quick intake of breath. Alive. Together. Communion. God. Lord God, from whom all life. More important than the wish we had forgotten. "Thank you, thank you, Lord, for everything I can see." [8] We began with "me," "us," but God had been there all along.

Looking back, I am astonished at all we did and felt together over a span of three weeks, but actually in only seven half-days. Hooray for God!

[8] *Hymns Hot and Carols Cool.* © 1967, Richard K. Avery and Donald S. Marsh.

3

Concepts through Music and Other Arts

A L T H O U G H a camp or vacation school does provide opportunity for learning values in family style as we have seen in the previous chapter, the "family" is limited in scope. Children need the total church fellowship where all ages meet in Christian community not only for worship and social gatherings but in teaching situations too. It was a rich experience for all concerned when a musician in her eighties brought her autoharp to the Primary Department in our church during the lessons on Egypt, and helped them learn the song, "Go Down, Moses."

Children also need a sense of continuity the *ad hoc* group cannot supply. They need to feel their "ground" steady enough to support growth and change. An inner-city child from a broken home in Cleveland used to appear at Calvary Church an hour before time for church school, needing a place where she could feel wanted and safe, a home for all seasons, the "Father's House." When the home situation was mended, she stopped coming early. A young girl who lived near Riverside Church in New York City said that when she could not sleep at night she would look out her window at the lighted church tower and be re-assured. A sense of security requires a sense of permanence and of place, and is essential to support the idea that God's concern for individuals is not for just a day. How many distraught people have found refuge from the noise and confusion of city streets in the quiet and the space of a church with an open door. Architecture with a human purpose. In a wider context, Jesus said, "In my Father's house are many mansions. I go to prepare a *place* for you." He knew that a sense of place can remove fear in death as well as in life.

When a place is enriched by the things we see and hear, the concepts they teach are enriched too. The country church as well as the cathedral has an organ or a piano and a special place for the choir, thus letting it be known that music is important there. Some have bells or chimes to celebrate the good news of God's love. At the New York Avenue Church in Washington, D.C., the Lincoln Chimes are rung just as the large Bible is brought in and placed on the pulpit. The "opening of the Bible" as it is called in the liturgy suggests the importance of the written Word, and the harmony of the chimes underlies the joy that the Word proclaims. It is a double affirmation and comes on strong at the beginning of a service of worship.

In the Abbey Church in Tewkesbury, England, stands the organ that John Milton played in the seventeenth century, an eloquent reminder that he contributed the art of music as well as poetry to the service of God. When he was twenty-one and a student at Christ College, Cambridge, he wrote "On the Morning of Christ's Nativity," a poem which states the central truth of Christian faith, that God actually came to live among us as a human being.

Cathedrals are not being built these days because the cost is prohibitive, and it is heartwarming to know that the Episcopal Church voted a few years ago to let the towers of St. John the Divine in New York City remain unfinished and give the money—something over two million dollars, I believe—to the needs of the poor. This does not mean we cannot make use of the remarkable variety of art already available in cathedrals, which can serve as a kind of library of "visual arts" for Christian education. There are symbols and stories in stained-glass windows, sculpture, tapestries, paintings, brass. Along the south wall of the Cathedral of St. John the Divine is an alcove containing a dramatic marble of the Prodigal Son on his knees. At Riverside Church there is a window the children helped to plan when the church was built. They chose the key quotation for the Bible window, "God is Love," and there it is, in several languages, etched in the jewel-like panes of glass. Near the choir-stalls in London's Westminster Abbey is a monument erected by black peoples in honor of William Wilberforce whose influence in Parliament helped to abolish the slave trade in the British colonies in 1807. I happened to be reading the inscription one Sunday when the Boys' Choir raised their voices at Evensong that made the spine tingle as the tones floated up to the Gothic vaulting high above.

If beauty in the church becomes an end in itself, we might have to forsake our buildings and take to the fields to worship. But when winter comes, where would be our place? Private homes can shelter small groups but not the gathered church that needs occasionally to assemble as a whole. Moreover, grass and clover are beautiful too, and could in turn become an idol. And you cannot bring gifts to adorn a field! I like what Pastor Avery said in his budget letter to the members of our church on "Why give?"

I love the building on the corner of Sussex and Broome Street, where all 120 years (and more) of faith and devotion are felt with its symbols and windows and echoes of

song and laughter and silence. . . . I want that building
to be there and to be used.

You know that love for a place of fellowship is catching
on when a teenage brother and sister bring home a beautiful
wooden chalice from Hawaii for the communion table in
Port Jervis, a young veteran returning from service in
Germany brings a crystal one from Augsburg, and a group
who visited Spain bring back one of silver. Even preschool
children can relate to this feeling for the church when
they sing:

> Our dear church was built
> with love and work and prayer,
> so that all the neighbors
> might find welcome there.[1]

They can sing it when a new picture is hung, or the walls
are painted, or when they tour the church to look at the
windows or the new lectern. It is so short and easy to sing
that it can be a spontaneous response to some surprise or
special happening if the teacher starts them off. The song
is also reprinted in *Songs for Early Childhood* published
by Westminster Press. Two other favorites to have ready
for special moments are "I Will Sing to the Lord as Long
as I Live"[2] and "Love One Another."[3]

Whatever the place of worship, music helps to keep
the heart sincere. There is a new song that reminds us that
the church is more than a building, and a person of any

[1] Reprinted by permission of the United Church Press from Danielson
and Conant, *Song and Play for Children.*

[2] By Jean H. Kremer, 1932, in *Songs and Hymns for Primary Children* (Philadelphia: Westminster Press, 1963).

[3] By Edith Sloane, in *Sing for Joy* (New York: Seabury Press, 1961).

age can sing it, or all ages together: "We Are the Church!" [4] Here is the chorus:

> I am the church!
> You are the church!
> We are the church together!
>
> All who follow Jesus
> All around the world
> Yes, we're the church together!

The last verse says loud and clear that all ages of people "belong":

> I count if I am ninety,
> or nine or just a baby:
> There's one thing I am sure about
> and I don't mean maybe:

[Repeat chorus]

Avery and Marsh were commissioned by the United Methodist Church to write the song for their curriculum, and no doubt each church has its own special way of doing it. This is the way we sing it at Port Jervis.

Each person chooses someone nearby for a partner. We sing the chorus first, and on the first line everyone points to himself, on the second, to his partner, and on the third the two shake hands. On the fourth, the arms are extended, on the fifth they describe a circle as big as the world, and on the last line partners come together again by linking arms or putting them around each other. The song can be sung several times, choosing a different partner each time

---

[4] © 1972, Richard K. Avery and Donald S. Marsh, from *Songs for the Easter People*. Used by permission.

without having to leave the pew. It is a joyous way of
being alive to your "belonging" and it can be done with
very little preparation even if it has never been tried before. Some say that as they look into each other's eyes on
the words, "You are the church," they realize, with something of a shock, how seldom they really "see" each other
in that light.

There may be times when the members of a church
school want to let the congregation know what it means
to them to belong to the church family. This happened
one spring in the First Presbyterian Church of Greenwich,
Connecticut, when Dr. John Bates was the senior minister.
He suggested a "recognition" service on a Sunday morning, one that would be a communication between church
and church school.

A group of representative parents, teachers, and children
as well as youth met with the director and talked it over.
Out of that came a liturgy with something for each age
group. The choir director helped with the music and each
department worked on their part of the project. The key
songs were "Lord, I Want to Be a Christian" and an African
mission song set to the music of a Liberian folktune,
"I Have Heard Good News Today." The Under-Twelves
were represented by three dialogues related to the preschool, the Primary, and Junior groups, and called "A
Family Talks It Over": Children Belong; Children Grow
in Christian Faith; Children Grow in Christian Responsibility. The youth groups presented a tape with conversation in their own voices representing well-known charac-
ters from the New Testament, and the Junior Choir
practiced leading a processional and a recessional hymn as
well as an anthem.

When infant baptism is included in a service, a good
song to try is "Father of the Human Family" by Walter

Henry Farquharson.[5] The second verse is of particular interest because of its reference to parents and their part in the sacrament:

> Grace and strength grant these young parents;
> of their call keep them aware;
> with your love surround these children,
> they your life of joy to share.

A shortcut to the concept of "family belonging" can be achieved for the entire congregation naturally and easily through a song. This happened in Port Jervis one Sunday when the Decker family gathered around the piano and sang a family anthem in which all six took part. Mom and Dad, Patti and Kenny divided the words among them, Kurt, the youngest, sat on the piano and rocked back and forth, Kelly stood in the aisle surveying the scene but apparently feeling very much a part of it. He sang now and then but his real contribution was a lusty "Amen" at the end, not provided for in the music. It happened to be his favorite word at the time and, I understand, the first word he ever said.

Teaching concepts through music or other arts in the church may take place incidentally, as we have seen, or through deliberate and careful planning. They may play a minor role, as when music sets the mood in a pantomime, or they may provide the germinating idea for an entire program. When a group of Primary children dramatized the story of Nehemiah with paperbag puppets, writing their own script, making the puppets, and using their own voices for the parts, they played a recording of "Kol Nidre" between scenes, the nearest thing to Hebrew music they could find at the time. Although it was not an

[5] From the Canadian hymnbook published jointly by the Anglican Church and the United Church of Canada, 1971.

integral part of the story, the music added color and feeling-tone and unified the scenes. Suppose a church were planning a community night: the committee might choose the hymn "O Brother Man" as the keynote for the evening and build the program around that. If there are Spanish-speaking neighbors, a calypso band might be available for special songs and dances, with a piñata for the children. Such evenings are often annual events in integrated congregations or ecumenical gatherings in urban areas.

When you are teaching in a church school, there is nothing more challenging than to see how meaningful you can make that brief period, not only for the children but for yourself as well. You don't want them to be bored and there is no good reason why *you* should be. Whether you start your planning in a committee or on a team or at your own kitchen sink is not so important as that those who do it are open to new ideas and willing to try them out.

Some of the biblical material is so rich in concepts that it can support a whole cluster of activity. The Egypt story is one of the best because it involves conflict, which is the essence of drama. Whether you decide to begin with Joseph and his jealous brothers and a benign ruler in Egypt, or with Moses and Pharoah who "knew not Joseph," there is always the third protagonist, the Other, who must be reckoned with eventually, the One True God.

The suggestions which follow have all been tried and tested at various times and places from Cleveland to Port Jervis. Not all would be practicable in all situations. It is best to keep plans simple, and focus on whatever part of the story is likely to have an impact that will be remembered and a concept *worth* remembering. Suppose you have already decided that you want to connect American folk music with the story of slavery in Egypt, partly at least because the Negro spirituals are an important part of

America's folk tunes. You will most certainly want to use "When Israel Was in Egypt Land," sometimes called "Go Down, Moses." You can begin with a bang and act out the basic conflict the first day or you can ease into it with a mural for background setting, and bring out the story as you go along, learning the song when you feel the right moment has arrived.

If you choose to begin with the basic conflict, no advance preparation is needed by the group as a whole. No script, no costumes, just the concept of a people under a heavy burden, needing to be free. You can call for volunteers to represent the slaves bearing their burden, the taskmaster standing on one side with a whip (use gestures rather than a real prop) and Moses on the other, seeing the situation and reacting. The "chain gang" can move about the room slowly in single file, heads bowed under the lash. A kind of rhythm will emerge if members of the group keep together by putting the right hand on the shoulder of the one in front, and then pausing in unison on each step. The first verse of the spiritual could be memorized at the end of the dramatization; but if it is learned first, then everyone can sing it as the slave scene is acted out. As a group grows more and more confident, scenes can be improvised with few suggestions from a leader except a statement of the situation.

When it comes to the scene of the burning bush and Moses' encounter with God, the teacher should be familiar with its source: the third chapter of Exodus and part of the fourth, selecting only the essential details to tell. Printed below is the story as we pared it down from thirty-four verses to only twenty-nine short lines. We printed these on a poster, those relating to God and His words in red, those for Moses in black. In the arrangement below, italics are used in place of red.

Now Moses was keeping the flock . . . and came to
  Horeb, the mountain of God.

And the angel of the Lord appeared to him
  in a flame of fire
  out of the midst of the bush

and he looked,
and lo, the bush was burning
yet it was not consumed.

God called to him out of the bush.
  "Moses, Moses!"

And he said, "Here am I."

Then he said," . . . *put off your shoes* . . .
  the place on which you are standing
  is holy ground."

And Moses hid his face,
  for he was afraid to look at God.

Then the Lord said
  "I have seen the affliction of my people
  and I have come . . . to deliver them
  Come, I will send YOU to Pharoah
  that you may BRING FORTH MY PEOPLE."

But Moses said
  "Who am I that I should go?
  I am slow of speech."

Then the Lord said
  Who has made man's mouth? Is it not I?
  Now therefore go

> *And I will teach you*
> *what you shall speak."*

After the group has heard the story, it can be posted for future reference or review, and the scene can be improvised.

From among those in Port Jervis who volunteered to represent Moses, we chose a girl because she had the qualities most likely to make the scene meaningful. To children accustomed to acting out stories on the spur of the moment, the logic of sex identity is no barrier to their imagination. If God can speak to a human being, the person who hears could be a man or a woman. I had had a short conference with her on how she could indicate that God's voice speaks through our thoughts, after which she stood before the group as Moses, speaking to God in her own words, then listening as she "heard" his voice:

I wish my people could be free.
(listens)

Who, ME? Oh, I couldn't.
(listens)

I can't talk all that good. I sort of stutter.
(listens)

Yes, I *know* it's important.
(listens)

You mean *YOU* will help me?"
(listens)

You really mean it?
(listening)

Well, then, I think I can do it. If you will help me.

We did several other dialogues, but this one held the attention of both the children and adults better than any of the others. Moses was beginning to seem like a real person, and since there was no costume to put a distance between him and themsleves, they could more readily get the point that God can speak to us today if we pay attention, and might even call us to bring freedom and justice to those who do not have it.

The second verse of a song written in 1964 would be a good one to learn at this point if the group does not already know it. The tune is one of Tallis's canons.

> It [the Bible] tells of your great love for all;
> Of men who answered to your call
> To trust in you and do your will
> Your loving purpose to fulfill.[6]

The group can also sing "Go Down Moses" and learn the last two verses even though they may not know the entire story yet.

We decided on pastel chalk and crayons for the burning bush artwork. The reverence and awe we had been feeling through the story, the song, and the dramatization of Moses' encounter with God, was translated by the children into the language of graphic art. From time to time all the children and youth had been drawn into the Moses project, and so on this morning, instead of painting in small class groups, we all worked together in the chapel. When the results of an intense period were put up for display, we were delighted with their color and movement, their quality of being alive. No two were alike. Kathy's bush crackled with the flame; Tom's was like a tree stand-

[6] "The Bible, God, Is Wise and True," in *Sing of Life and Faith.* Words copyright, 1965, by the United Church Press. Used by permission.

ing in lush green grass; Joe and Brad both indicated a scene of mystery, but Donna's fire came from the heart of the bush in a desert setting; Debbie was the only one who included Moses; Bonna the only one who used her 12 x 18 paper vertically; Sandi drew a sun in one corner and a moon in the other (the bush burns night and day?); Patti did an unusual design of bush and flame; Richard a blend of sky with bush and fire; Sue, a bush that matched the sun in intensity, and so on.

> There's a fire within us O Lord,
> A new life's a burnin' O Lord,
> A fire for new life,
> Combating present strife,
> There's a fire within us, O Lord.[7]

"The Church Within Us" is a favorite of our youth choirs, and although it is a New Testament subject, the roots of the Church began in the Old Testament, so why not relate the concept of the burning bush to our own hearts now?

We know from the fifteenth chapter of Exodus that after the Israelites had passed safely through the waters, Moses led the men—and his sister Miriam, the women— in a song of triumphant praise sometimes called the "Song of the Sea," sometimes "Song to the Eternal." Miriam and the women used timbrels (the biblical word for tambourines) to accompany their singing and dancing:

> I will sing to the Lord, for he has triumphed gloriously;
>   the horse and his rider he has thrown into the sea.
> The Lord is my strength and my song,
>   and he has become my salvation;

[7] By Kent Schneider, in *Songbook for Saints and Sinners*, edited by Carlton Young. Published by Agape Press, 1971. Used by permission.

> this is my God, and I will praise him,
>   my father's God and I will exalt him.

Exodus 15:1-2

This could be represented in a worship service by two groups, one to chant the words and the other to dance with tambourines. It would be fun to follow it with the contemporary "Passed Thru the Waters" [8] which could be sung by both choir and congregation. It is a song with a vigorous beat that delighted our 1971 Confirmation Class to whom it is dedicated:

> Like survivors of the Flood,
> Like walkers thru the sea,
> Like walkers thru the God-divided sea:
> We are rescued, we are claimed,
> We are loved and we are named,
>
>   We are baptized!
>   I am baptized!
>   We have passed thru the waters
>   And that's all that matters!
>   We have passed thru the waters!
>   O thanks be to God!

The congregation as a whole responds to it with enthusiasm, especially when the drums take part. The composers suggest that the song be sung with "joy and fervor . . . with clapping, shouting, and other Biblical acts." Let anyone who fears that shouting is no way to praise God read the account in Ezra of the celebration at the laying of the foundation of the new Temple when the Hebrews returned from exile. The priests blew trumpets, the Levites beat their hand drums and sang responsively, while "all the

[8] © 1971, Richard K. Avery and Donald S. Marsh. From *Alive and Singing*. Used by permission.

people shouted with a great shout when they praised the Lord . . . and the sound was heard afar" (Ezra 3:11-12).

They say that on rising, Martin Luther put his hand on his head and said, "I am baptized!" We all do this at our church when we have a baptism and when we come to "I am baptized" in the song. When we have visitors they join in too. One day we had a guest from the staff of the rare-book room of a great library, who said with tears in her eyes after the service, "They certainly know how to move you here!"

After we completed the unit on Moses, we made a time-line of biblical history as it relates to the Church, developing it by centuries to help visualize the way God works through people and crises. Don Marsh was inspired when he suggested we make it one-, two-, and three-dimensional and hang it on a heavy clothesline across the chapel from wall to wall. So we did. No timid clinging by a string to a parochial bulletin board. No monotonous series of dates. They were there, but animated by symbols, pictures, children's paintings, textured signs to point up events. For the fall of Rome, for instance, there was a cluster of rubble dangling under A.D. 410, along with a small sign reading LAW, another GOOD ROADS, another ABILITY TO ORGANIZE. We did our dramatization along the way under the appropriate date. For example, Moses had the talk with God that changed the history of the world between two swinging signs that read:

SLAVERY IN EGYPT	EXODUS
400 years	1290 B.C.

Along the clothesline from end to end, we also stretched a bright red ribbon to represent the love of God in continuous action throughout both the Old and New Testa-

ments. Now and then signs like those above called attention to certain facts, sometimes reassuring, sometimes horrifying: 300 YEARS' PERSECUTION; CONSTANTINE CONVERTED;
DARK AGES—500 YEARS; ST. AUGUSTINE GOES TO ENGLAND;
CRUSADES—SLAUGHTER OF THOUSANDS SPONSORED BY CHRIS-
TIANS; and so on. Richard Avery was inspired when he
used symbols in the chancel during a sermon series on
"Heroes of the Faith A.D.," such as a fishnet for Peter, a
saddle for the Presbyterian circuit rider Mackemie, a
window for Pope John to "open" to the world, Luther's
hammer for nailing his ninety-six theses to the church door.
These symbols enriched what the children were doing in
the church school, for numbers of them do attend, the
youth choirs always. This is one of the bonuses in a family-
oriented church.

Martin Luther was represented on the time-line by a
full-length portrait of a monk painted by a Junior, and on
Reformation Sunday we sang Luther's masterpiece, "A
Mighty Fortress Is Our God." He wrote both words and
music and is credited with publishing a hymnbook of
twenty-three hymns of his own.

Luther evidently had a beautiful voice and enjoyed
singing. Like many other students of his day, he sang in the
streets to help earn his way through school. A motherly
woman, Frau Cotta, was so taken with the quality of his
voice in the church choir as well as on the streets, that
she offered him a home as a sort of foster son. It endears
him to us that he did not develop the stern attitudes of the
puritans but wanted children to laugh and play, and encouraged young people to sing and dance and put on
shows. He himself had feared God when he was a child
and he was concerned that other children know him in a
relationship of love. To quote one of his hymns: "Teach
us to know our God aright, and call him father from the
heart." I was glad to discover that this hymn, "Come, Holy

Spirit, God and Lord," [9] is harmonized by J. S. Bach. Since it is based on a medieval antiphon, it would be fun to try it antiphonally in relation to Luther's story.

Children enjoy choosing scenes from Luther's life story to paint, like the moment in the storm when he vowed to become a monk if he were not struck by lightning, or the nailing of the ninety-six theses to the church door, or the kidnaping incident, or the trial for heresy. A fourth-grade boy chose to paint Luther taking his stance of courage at the trial. He called it "Here I Stand, God Help Me."

Both children and adults like to dramatize an imaginary press conference with a favorite in church history. Some knowledge of the person to be interviewed is of course a necessary preparation, but dialogue will be more natural when it is improvised rather than learned. Freedom to take the risk of not knowing in advance exactly what other persons involved are going to say is part of the fun and likely to make the scene more creative for both actors and audience. In one church where both costumes and a script were used for such an interview, one of the actors was criticized by a fellow member because his robe had been an inch too short to cover the bottom of his trousers. Today we are more interested in what a St. Francis or a Pope John can say to us than in the length of their robes, which is another reason why, except in formal drama, costumes are out of date these days in religious education.

In Port Jervis just before Lent we tried an experiment in understanding with a Junior High class. Without preparation, we listened as a group to a recording of "Vincent," the song based on the life of van Gogh which happened to be popular in the area at the time. Then I asked them what it meant to them. Apparently very little. After I told them the story of his life, showing the prints of some of his

[9] In *Hymns for Junior Worship* (Philadelphia: Westminster Press, 1966).

paintings to point up the main events and the growth in his art, paintings that were little recognized until after his tragic death, we played the record a second time. The reaction of the class was entirely different. There were questions and comments, but best of all, expressions of compassion and concern for his disappointments and frustrations. They understood the song now and were ready to respond with words and feelings of compassion. When a copy of "Vincent's" painting "The Starry Night' was given to each member of the class to take home, expressions of appreciation were meaningful too. During the period of Lent which followed, I believe we were more open to the impact of those forty days on Jesus' life in Palestine and on us today than we would have been without the artist's story and the song about him.

Anyway, we plunged into the task of getting the events of that fateful period straight in our minds and then tackled the meaning for our own lives later. When we discovered how many happenings involved words beginning with the letter "P" we made that a focus just for the fun of it, putting a huge capital "P" on the bulletin board and surrounding it with signs made of construction paper in bright colors, each bearing one of the "P" words in large letters: Palestine, Parables, People, Prince of Peace, Pilate, Peter, Priests, Pharisees, Passover, Passion Week, and so on, with Pentecost to come later. Since many of the Junior Highs were in the youth choir, these girls and boys were learning songs all along that related to our class activity. They were also hearing the songs presented by the Adult Choir, so that they were exposed to a wide range of music for Lent. The spirituals "Lonesome Valley," "Let Us Break Bread Together," and "Were You There?"; the African "Kum Ba Yah"; "I Wonder Why" and "Here He Comes" by Avery and Marsh; "Lord of Passover, Pity, and Sorrow" arranged by Paul Abels; "Bitter Was the Night" by Sidney

Carter; Gene MacClellan's "Put Your Hand in the Hand"; and Charles A. Tindley's "Stand By Me"; in addition to the works of composers ranging from Bach to Benjamin Britten.

As Good Friday approached, we tried to come to grips with two of the most important concepts for Lent: Penitence and Pardon. For penitence we shared what we might want to repent of—feel sorry for—and one of the girls volunteered to demonstrate how the body could say, "I'm sorry." First she got down on her knees, then touched the floor with her forehead. Then everyone tried modeling a penitent figure from homemade clay. The figures showed a surprising amount of feeling and no two were alike. The next week we followed up with conversation on what it means to be forgiven. We recalled Jesus' parable of the Forgiving Father (Prodigal Son) and how complete his love was for the wandering son whose homecoming called for a celebration. We modeled clay figures again to show the joy of being pardoned, of being together again after separation. We were so pleased with them we displayed them in the chapel together with the "I am sorry" figures.

One day when the sun was right, we arranged the "penitents" at the foot of the big tree behind the church. There

was still some ice and snow symbolizing the cold of sin
and death and sadness, but the strong roots of the tree
showed through like the power of God's forgiving love.
When spring came, we took a second photograph, this
time of the pardoned people rejoicing with the flowers.

During the last week before Easter, the rugged cross
made from two trees was brought into the sanctuary and
on Palm Sunday one of the men sang a solo, standing
beneath it and looking up. He sang it slowly and dramati-
cally and unaccompanied. Three of the verses are quoted
below:

> O God, O Son of God,
> what is this sight I see?
> In the blindness of the moment
> I have nailed you to a tree.

O God, O Son of God,
receive my humble prayer
and accept my sin which I confess
and which you say you bear.

O God, O Son of God,
I make this solemn vow:
That just as you gave your life for me
I'll live mine for you now.[10]

I wish that the two boys who caused such anguish to a third on the playground of our summer class had been there. The arts can reach deep into human consciousness, and if a bully could just once really hear a light-bearing song, it might stay with him even if he tries to forget it along with the "holy hunger" of his heart. Some times I wonder what might have happened in *Lord of the Flies* if one of the boys had started to sing.

Even after Easter that year our church family kept on experiencing the wonders and the symbols of spring. On the fifth Sunday of Eastertide our worship was still bursting with it. The organ prelude was "The Peaceful Forests" by Isaak, the Offertory was "Spring Song" by Lucas, the Postlude was Beethoven's "The Glory of God in Nature," the first hymn was "This Is My Father's World," and the youth choir sang "Celebration" by Dunn and Green. As usual, the responses for the liturgy were original:

The sun breaks through!
BIRDS SING AGAIN!

The green blade rises!
FLOWERS SPROUT, and
BUDS ARE ON THE TREES!

[10] © 1971, Richard Avery and Donald S. Marsh. From *Alive and Singing*. Used by permission.

Children on bicycles
laugh down the street!
OLDER FOLKS STROLL IN
THE SUNSHINE AND SMILE!

Spring is here!
GOD RULES THE WORLD!
The Lord is risen!
THE LORD IS RISEN INDEED. ALLELUIA!

It was a joyous crowning of the concept that pardon follows penitence, which we had been molding in clay and
hopefully also in ourselves, and it happened without a
committee meeting. Partly because we are a family church
and all ages rub elbows in their learning, partly because
there is a Holy Spirit.

But lest we as a covenant people become sentimental
about spring, the anthem that day was a salty one, "God
Is Working His Purpose Out," [11] including the challenge,
"What can we do to hasten the day . . . that shall find us
living in peace," and ending with the warning, "time is
running out." The closing hymn was "Rise Up, O Men of
God."

To mention one more concept we worked on that spring:
the Christian has a right to hope and the privilege of spreading it. It happened that the offering that year from the
"One Great Hour of Sharing" was to go for self-development in India and Africa as well as areas in the United
States, and the theme was to be "Here's Hope". So on the
same Sunday described above, the Liturgy of Concern included preparation for the annual worldwide sharing.
Members of the Presby Players drama workshop improvised scenes of need, and women from the diaconate

[11] Carlton Young, in *Songbook for Saints and Sinners* (Chicago:
Agape Press, 1971).

offered prayers for the Church and the world. The next week the symbol of a rainbow appeared on the chancel wall and large posters made by the Junior Highs showed up at the rear of the church announcing the One Great Hour of Sharing with pictures of hungry children, a green earth, a cross, clasped hands, a rainbow. "Love Is Persistent Concern" said one caption, another "Waiting," and a third, under a copy of a stern portrait of Christ,[12] "He Don't Mean Maybe!"

Children of the church school painted pictures in response to their own ideas of hope in the world: Kenny's "Hope for the World" was a large green earth filling his paper; Ellen's "Hope for Fish," a fisherman in a boat, "but all the fish are dead because the water is polluted" (there they were, lying on their backs on the beach, fins up!); Gessner's "Hope for Flowers"—only two left alive; Cheryl's positive note, "Hope Is Singing," showed three children striding toward the church and all singing.

When sharing day finally arrived, all the things the church school students had been making were on display around the chapel to celebrate hope and spring, and the presence of the Holy Spirit, whose day it was. To have Pentecost coincide with One Great Hour of Sharing was a lot for one day. "Thank you, thank you, Lord."

On the following Sunday, when we learned that our offering for self-development around the world had soared to a sum two hundred dollars more than had ever before been received in our church for One Great Hour of Sharing, we saw that hope had been justified. The rainbow of promise we had painted in the sky was beginning to show itself on earth.

[12] "Head of the Christ" by the contemporary American artist Wieczerek.

Thank you, thank you, thank you, thank you Lord,
for everything that we are,
A chosen people who have wandered far,
By your grace
Here we are:
Grateful for our lives upon this little star.
Thank you, thank you, my Lord.[13]

[13] © 1967, Richard K. Avery and Donald S. Marsh. From *Hymns Hot and Carols Cool.* Used by permission.

SUMMARY OF CONCEPTS PRESENTED IN THIS CHAPTER

I. The Church
   is a place

                    you can count on
                    to love and take care of
                    where you learn to know about
                    God and Jesus and hopefully, learn
                    to know *them*
   is a fellowship

                    of love
                    for all ages
                    like a family
   has ups and downs

                    as in the time-line and art, drama,
                    music (Moses, Jesus, Luther)
   has crises of faith

                    as in the Reformation
II. Bible Stories
    Faith drama

                    The Hebrews are rescued from
                       slavery
                    Jesus shows God's love (Lent,
                       Passion Week)

Meanings
    Old Testament
           God knows what we're up against
           He acts to rescue us
           He speaks to us if we listen
             (Moses)
           He may ask people to lead who
             don't think they qualify
           He keeps His promises and means
             people to keep theirs
             (Covenant)
    New Testament
           Penitence
           Pardon
           Hope
III. Hope can be fulfilled
    Caring
    Sharing ("One Great Hour" Offering)
IV. Learning from Life
    Vincent van Gogh
    Understanding
    Compassion

4
Celebrate to Remember

S O M E O N E has said, "No music, no church." Certainly there cannot be much of a celebration without music and this was one of John Calvin's problems. He had good reason to celebrate but dared not encourage music beyond the psalm tunes for fear of risking frivolity. For some time now denominations have been moving toward the freedom to borrow from each other's traditions or experiment with new forms or mix the two, and the results are encouraging. Some of the changes began very quietly as far back as the transformation of "Children's Day." Giving children "pieces to speak" gradually gave way in some churches to an hour-long service of worship in which all departments presented a recapitulation of the year's work. Samplings of class conversations, tableaus, choral speaking of Scripture, and songs by all age groups were held together by narrators and the adult choir. Several rather unusual occasions of this sort were worked out in the New York Avenue Presbyterian Church in Washington, D.C., using Hebrew cantillation, ancient "Yigdal" melody, as well as familiar songs from Kindergarten up. The theme of the worship was whatever it had been in the church school for the year, possibly the church, the Bible, or the life of Christ, and these occasions required and received the full cooperation of both the minister, Dr. George Docherty, and Stephen Prussing, the choir director. Departments rehearsed separately and came together just once for a final run-through. This was a formal presentation without improvising, an innovation whose value many of us had not yet discovered. Even so, it was creative because it involved the planning as well as the participation of numbers of people.

Another change in celebration styles has come in what at first seemed quite shocking to some—the use of dance in worship. A wholesome trend has been to move away from "importing" professional performers, for one special occasion, to developing a rhythm choir from members of the congregation or church school, and combining it with choral singing. At Riverside Church in New York City we were fortunate one year to have a professional dancer work with Primary and Junior children in the summer vacation school. They were delighted with his concept of dancing, "sculpturing in space," and still more pleased with having an important part in the closing service of praise in Christ Chapel. Along with songs, prayers, and Scripture presented by other children, the dancers developed simple movements for an "Introit" at the beginning and a "Benediction" at the end. In between they preached a sermon! Five or six children sat in a circle on the stone floor in front of the altar, and one after the other stood up, gave a "message" in movement, and sat down. When all had "spoken," they joined hands and skipped in a circle.

Another year we praised God at the end of the summer through music and art: a fun-song and several hymns of praise we had learned, a trumpet solo by one of the Puerto Rican boys, and an exhibit of the children's paintings. The school had been divided into four groups and each chose what parts of praise it would be responsible for. Because we had seen a documentary film on the life of Helen Keller, we decided that an offering to help blind people would be our closing act of praise. Since the service was in a classroom that year instead of in the chapel, the paintings were on the walls all around us, adding their own colorful kind of music to the worship.

"What about Thanksgiving?" someone asks. In Port Jervis we have a family dinner at the church on Sunday night preceding the holiday and sing hymns and songs around the tables afterward. Communitywise, we have an ecumenical celebration sponsored by the Ministerial Association. When it is at the synagogue, all the men wear yamulkas, and the ministers from the various churches walk down the center aisle in their robes and yarmulkes with the rabbi to take their places on the platform. It is beautiful to see them sitting up there on either side of the bronze symbol of the burning bush, and taking turns with the prayers and the talks.

When the service was at the Presbyterian Church, half an hour before the service was to begin, the chapel was crowded with participants rehearsing, checking their robes and music, admiring the trombone of the new choirmaster in town, who was to make his debut that evening. Then the host minister took his place by the door and prayed. We were ready to go in.

Since part of the service was to be a Festival of Psalms, the rabbi had consented to sing one in Hebrew. The congregation was moved by the extraordinary quality and power of his voice, evidently trained and experienced in the art of chant. Our minister "lined out" another psalm, leading the congregation in singing and speaking antiphonally. One of the youth choirs sang a number with delicate accompaniment of finger cymbals and a triangle, the

Orff group came in on the drums, and the combined adult choirs really did themselves proud in "Let All Things Now Living" in vigorous drinking-song rhythm. The mayor was present on the platform to read the President's Proclamation. Later we sang "He's Got the Whole World in His Hand" and Richard Avery led us in ad-lib verses from time to time. During the sharing of personal reasons for being thankful, the Lutheran minister, whose little daughter had been killed by a car a few months before, mentioned that since his wife could not have another child, they were adopting one soon. Then the words of the song became, "He's got the new little daughter in His hand" and the congregation picked it up. At another point the minister ad libbed, "He's got the City of Port Jervis in His hand" and gave the mayor, who was standing next to him, a friendly little nudge as if to say, "How *about* that!"

When Christmas comes, people can forget their differences and sing carols. Even those who like to argue, "If Luther didn't write 'Away in a Manger,' who did?" will ultimately stop talking and sing it instead. Everyone seems to like carols, perhaps because their unaffected joy tells so clearly the message of the Incarnation.

In the preface to his collection of songs, *Faith, Folk and Nativity*, Peter Smith, a Methodist minister in Sheffield, England, gives a brief but informative history of the Christmas carol. He thinks it may go back to the Greek *choras*, a dance done in a circle, picking up further life from the thirteenth-century troubadour songs and becoming its most creative in the fifteenth and sixteenth centuries as a festive song related to Christmas. Almost lost to many Christians during the Puritan days but reestablished in the nineteenth century, they are quite indispensable to Christmas celebrations. It was his early training as a pianist and his later world travel which stimulated Peter Smith's interest in the roots of musical expression in a variety of cultures. This Christmas collection includes folk carols of many origins such as Welsh, Irish, Silesian, Chinese, as well as English, American, and the Negro Spiritual. One of our favorites in Port Jervis is the first song in the book, "Every Star Shall Sing a Carol," by Sidney Carter.

Carols can be teamed with an exciting variety of events, a family party for instance, where moms and dads and children make Christmas cards together, or a crèche or clay figures to go in it (clothespins and pipestem cleaners if you don't have clay). At one such evening at the New York Avenue Church in Washington, D. C., the handicapped children from the Saturday church school class which was held that year showed the slides which they had posed in their own room to illustrate the Christmas story. "Mary" was in a wheel chair. Then they came as honor guests to the Peter Marshall Hall, where not all of them could make things with their hands but they could sing carols, and enjoyed being at a regular party with other people, especially when their contribution to the performance received its share of applause. The children's choir sang "The Christmas Candle" by Roberta Bitgood, the Youth Fellowship gave a Christmas pantomime, and a Japanese-American boy sang "O Holy Night."

On Christmas Eve, at eleven, carols were sung again, this time to introduce the reading of a play by Stephen Vincent Benét, "A Child Is Born". The moment of truth came just before the Lincoln chimes truck twelve, when a thief, who has seen the child in the stable, asks the innkeeper's wife if the child is for him too. When she assures his that he is, the thief probes more deeply, wanting to know if the child has come to all of us. "To every man alive," is her reply.[1]

At another church, the First Presbyterian in Greenwich, Connecticut, the carol singing came *after* a chancel play-

---

[1] Thelma Sherman Brown, ed., *Treasury of Religious Plays* (New York: Association Press, 1947).

reading. "The Holy Family" by W. H. Ward is a verse drama that requires neither costumes nor memorizing and combines the old story with the modern scene and the human dilemma that is true of both. Early in the play the people are saying: "And now for us is the season of hope", but later, when they become aware of the demands Christ will make:

> . . . do not lay on us the burden of too much joy.
> . . . not for us the strange uncertainty,
> The leap in the dark.
> We do not ask for change. . . .
> We ask to remain unnoticed. Leave us in peace.[2]

Before they left for home, each family was given a hand-made booklet with carols and a worship service to use at home on Christmas Eve. It was arranged so that everyone in the family could have something special to do in addition to singing, like lighting a candle, reading verses from the Christmas story, a poem, or a prayer.

The older children and young people in this same church created an original worship service for their parents' guest day the Sunday morning before Christmas. In preparation they put together costumes—"not a bathrobe in the bunch!" —posed the Nativity scenes which one of the fathers photographed in color, and wrote a worship sequence, with the help of the director of education, which included Scripture and prayers and Christmas hymns as well as their colored slides. After working for good enunciation, they taped the sequence, leaving spaces for the hymns they would be singing with their parents. When the morning came, they greeted their guests proudly and took charge of the service, synchronizing the projector and the tape with the

---

[2] W. H. Ward, *The Holy Family* (London: The Religious Drama Society/SPCK). Used by permission.

piano and the singing. Part of the "good news" that day was their own growing sense of responsibility and achievement.

For a number of years during the sixties at Riverside Church, families of the church school came early on the Sunday before Christmas and worshiped together through a liturgy of music and drama, Scripture, prayer, and movement. Led by the organ and the combined choirs of youth and children in the chancel, and the handbells in the second balcony, the "family" congregation worshiped God and shared their joy with each other.

Sometimes between music and pantomime a family would interpret their own Christmas thoughts in a conversation at the front of the church. A portion of one such conversation is quoted below as it was created in advance by a professor at Union Seminary, his wife and daughter, and the director of Children's Work. Following a Christmas hymn, the family are talking about the meaning of Advent and the need for a strong leader felt by the ancient Hebrews:

Mother: But when the leader came, he was not the mighty king they had imagined him to be, was he?
Child: No, he was only a little baby.
Father: But he grew up to be a man.
Mother: And he did lead the people, only differently.
Child: How do you mean?
Father: With love and forgiveness, instead of swords and armies.
Mother: And Mary was the one chosen to be the mother.
  (*Mary enters, carrying a flower, sits on a low stool*)
Child: I remember. An Angel of the Lord told her she would have a very special baby. What is an "angel of the Lord"?
Mother: We think of an angel as a messenger.

Child: Oh yes, with wings.

Mother: Artists often draw angels with wings, although there is no place in the Bible where they are described that way.

Father: The important thing is this: whenever we read the words, "angel of the Lord," we must pay close attention because it means that God is very near.

At this point, the voices of the choir respond softly with the words from the Liturgy of St. James in the melody of an old French carol:

> Let all mortal flesh keep silence,
> And with fear and trembling stand;
> Ponder nothing earthly minded,
> For with blessing in his hand,
> Christ our God to earth descendeth,
> Our full homage to demand.

The service continues with the Annunciation and the Magnificat, a shepherd pantomime and "Sing Gloria" by the choir. Then this further family exchange:

Child: Were the shepherds in the story all grown-up people?

Mother: I presume many of them were, because the work was hard. The nights would be long and cold, and there was always the danger of wolves coming to attack the sheep.

Child: But wouldn't some children like me go along for a little while? In the daytime, maybe?

Father: I think they would. You can imagine that some of them may have been just about your own age!

For the birth scene at the crèche, both the youth and children's choirs sang the Lullaby, "Little Jesus, Sweetly Sleep" and finished with a song which at that time was an annual custom: "On This Day" by Gustav Holst. In these ways the story of our faith is handed on, through music and other arts, including the art of conversation! It is especially interesting to learn that the child in the conversation, who wanted so much to be a part of things, including the work of the shepherds, is now in Kenya on a graduate fellowship to study the place of women in an African society.

The next year at Riverside Church we presented the angels "nonverbally". That term was not yet in current use; we just thought that three barefoot angels, junior size, could say something beautiful about Jesus in rhythm, and when they moved around the crèche in a dance of adoration while the organist played Bach's "Jesu, Joy of Man's Desiring," it was the high moment of the worship that morning. During rehearsals we had taken several pictures of the angels enjoying each other's company, not knowing that one of the photographs might find its way to Russia.

It happened that in the spring a party from the Russian Orthodox Church in Moscow visited Riverside and we gave one of the pictures to a woman in the party, calling attention to the fact that children of three different races were having a good time together. We hoped that the photograph would carry back to Russia a message of a dream that is possible for America and the whole world. It was only later that we learned that the attractive young woman to whom we had given the picture was the wife of the Politburo member of the group. Surely he would not consider the angels subversive when they crossed the Russian border?

Peter Smith says, also in the preface mentioned earlier, that the fresh interest of the church in carol singing and carol services has caught on in England. "We are now faced," he says, "with the surprising sight, in this age of decline of religious observance, of carol services being celebrated to full churches, carol concerts being performed before packed enthusiastic audiences, and homes, pubs and clubs echoing their joyful refrains." [3] . ‾

The carol service has become increasingly popular in America too. In its purest form it is a simple presentation of the Christmas story through the reading of Scripture and the singing of carols. The Scripture is divided into episodes, each followed by a carol that relates to it. A modified form of the carol service was presented in Greenwich, Connecticut, years ahead of its time, at the First Presbyterian Church under the direction of the Rev. Richard Manzalmann. To the biblical narrative and the carols he added living pictures of Mary and Joseph, the shepherds and the kings. The carolers were all older children or members of the Youth Group who liked to sing. The choice of carols worked out with the choir director was a lively one, as shown in the program below.

[3] From the Preface to *Faith, Folk and Nativity*, edited by Peter Smith. © 1968 by Galliard Ltd. Used by permission.

PRELUDE: Variations on Italian Carols .... Berlioz
PROCESSIONAL HYMN: It Came Upon the
    Midnight Clear .... Carol
INTROIT: Welcome, Yule .... Eric Gritton
THE COMING FORETOLD:
    Now Tell Us, Gentle Mary, What Did
    Gabriel Say .... French
THE SHEPHERDS IN THE FIELDS:
    Carol of the Sheep Bells .... Kountz
    Shepherds, Shake Off Your Drowsy Sleep French
THE CHILD IS BORN:
    When the Herds Were Watching ...... English
    Sleep, My Jesus, Sleep .... Dutch
THE SHEPHERDS ADORE: The Birds .. Czech
THE KINGS ADORE:
    The March of the Kings (in the form
    of a round) .... Provencal
THE WORLD REJOICES:
    O Come Little Children .... Schultz
    Unto Us a Boy Is Born .... German
RECESSIONAL HYMN: Joy to the World Antioch

Those who are concerned with developing family events will be interested to know this service was scheduled for five o'clock on the Sunday preceding Christmas instead of at midnight so that the children could all come. It was followed by family festivities in three different rooms to accommodate everyone, each room with a tree, a piano and carol songbooks, a storyteller, and refreshments. Before leaving, each family was given a decoration from the tree to take home.

Every year on the Sunday night before Christmas, a Carol Caravan sets forth from our church in Port Jervis to serenade those who are ill or unable to go out to festivities. First there is a special program in the chapel, then cars and station wagons warm up their motors, the carolers get aboard, and the caravan winds its way to the first stop. We don't go in, but stand facing the house and start to sing. People come to the door or window and wave, if they are able, but don't suggest coming in because they know there are others waiting for us. When the last carol has been sung to the last people on our list, everyone goes to "Betty's house" for hot chocolate and homemade cookies.

For the preliminary program in the chapel one year, we gave an original play with everything from an Old Testament quarrel to a shepherd's pipe and a policeman's whistle. Our songs spanned the centuries too: an ancient plainsong, an eighteenth-century hymn, and a modern carol. The Holy Family was a young couple with their own infant son, and as children in the front row crowded around the crèche to see and adore, children of the choir led off with "Happy Birthday to You," ending with one of our best-loved carols:

> Mary, Mary, what you gonna name that baby?
> What you gonna call that ho-o-ly baby?
>
> Slaves are we and looking for a master,
> Why don't you call him Lord? Sh! [*finger on lips*]
> Let's all call him Lord![4]

Soloists in the group each took a turn singing one of the four stanzas, and everyone came in on the "Sh" and the words that follow, as well as the beginning two lines. We sang the song as a part of the play, and the closing lines were the goodnight lines of the master of ceremonies:

> As we go out now to sing for the shut-ins, let's all remember that since that first Christmas, *every* family is a holy family!

[4] © 1967, Richard K. Avery and Donald S. Marsh. "Mary, Mary," in *Hymns Hot and Carols Cool.* Used by permission.

For the caravan send-off one year, a group called the Genesis Singers, ages eight to twelve, presented a cantata, *The Christmas Jazz,* one of the new English series by Lloyd and Chappell. It is a contemporary version of the Bethlehem story seen through the eyes of the animals and shepherds, a colorful and humorous frolic featuring, among others, the donkey who furnished transportation and a centurion who had trouble with all those Hebrew names —the son of the son of the son of—parts to which Kathy and Brad gave just the right degree of dignity and comedy required. The musical is also beautiful and moving, with Mary and Joseph and the angels, wise men and shepherds and three "shivering sheep." Cynthia, as Mary, accompanied herself with finger cymbals as she sang the magnificat. Traditional and modern words mingle in the songs, notably in one sung by a shepherd: "Wake Up, I think I see an angel," and the cantata closes with the ancient lovely words, "Gloria in excelsis Deo."

Choirs can also serve a community by singing in hospitals, homes for the elderly, shopping malls, hotel lobbies. When you "celebrate to remember" it is good to remember to share. Both children and adults in our choirs here enjoy spreading the Good News together, and never more so than when invited to take a singing trip to a church in another town. In fact, such a trip has become a tradition here during the Advent season. The journey by chartered bus is filled with laughter and song, and the exchange with new friends a meaningful experience in Christian fellowship. The year we drove eighty-five miles in the snow and sang, among other songs, the wistful *Has Anybody Seen Christmas?, Jazz Gloria* with percussion, and *This Little Babe* as a duet with the choir humming in the background, topping it off with a hilarious *"Twelve Days of Christmas."* We were moved by the comment of our host as we took our departure: "We have never had so much joy under our roof before."

In one sense, Christians celebrate the Resurrection every Sunday at worship, but some of the special days through the year are more vividly remembered. A recent Palm Sunday in Port Jervis is one of those, when music, Scripture, and pantomime were combined to teach a lesson on God's grace. Five stories from the Bible were condensed and presented with a musical background of organ and piano while the congregation sang "Amazing Grace." Three of the stories were parables: the Lost Sheep, the Lost Coin, and the Prodigal Son. The other two were about Bartimaeus and Zaccheus and how each was healed, seemingly of different problems, yet alike in being preoccupied with money until Jesus came along.

As the key verses in the New Testament were read for each story, the actors, who were children as well as adults of varying ages, improvised the appropriate movements and gestures across the front of the church or down the aisles until given a signal to "freeze" like a statue. When all five stories had been "told," the congregation rose and sang again the first verse:

> Amazing grace! how sweet the sound,
> That saved a wretch like me!
> I once was lost, but now am found,
> Was blind but now I see.[5]

The anthem for the day was "Here He Comes," [6] written especially for Palm Sunday with the "triumphant" entry of Jesus in mind.

---

[5] © 1973, John Newton, in *Genesis Songbook*, published by Agape Press, Carol Stream, Ill. Used by permission.

[6] © 1970, Richard K. Avery and Donald S. Marsh. *Songs for the Easter People*. Used by permission.

Here he comes, the one we've heard so much about!
People point and push and jump and rush about!
Welcome! Welcome! Welcome to our town!
Great to have someone like you around!

Things'll get done,
Things'll get brighter,
Life'll be fun,
Life'll be lighter.
Say goodbye to sorrow,
He is our tomorrow,
He will make the old world fresh and new here.

At this point the choir divides, one section praising Jesus as above, the other opposing. It is a "brassy" conflict of enthusiasm and violent rejection, neither side comprehending the true state of affairs:

Who does he think he is?
He's arousing all the people,
Who does he think he is?
He'll take over church and steeple!
Get him out of town!
Get him on the run!
Get him with a sword or get him with a gun!
Stop him any way,
Any way we can!
He is nothing special, just another man!

At the end of the song, both groups join in the following irony,

WHAT COULD GO WRONG IN SPRING!

To answer that question with unmistakable clarity, comes the next song, "Blood," [7] designed to be sung by the

[7] *Ibid.*

leader and echoed by the people, phrase by phrase. There
is no accompaniment and the pace is slow, the feeling
dramatic, and the song tells it like it is: "Blood, life's blood,
red and real . . . beneath the cross . . . pours like wine, spills
in the dust, and so it must, for this is the way of truth and
love." The second verse comes closer: "My blood, red and
good, will it be spilling some day in such a way? For this
is the way of love, the way of truth and love."

·This is a strong song for children who may be present,
but we live in a world where strength is needed, and the
truth is best taught when children are surrounded by love
and understanding. This song is sung sorrowfully, in reverence and awe, in contrast to the shallow and brassy
moods of the preceding one. There is nothing morbid about
it because words and music are in harmony. Had the
tunes been reversed, both songs would have been false
and useless for Christian education. I am coming to see
that in trying to shield children from learning too much
too soon, we may have given them too little too late. In
wanting to avoid giving them a false sense of guilt, we have
encouraged them in a false sense of security that can throw
them when the big tests come. I would not plan a lesson
for a Primary Department around that song, but when it is
heard in the context of the gathered family, like anything
heard in a home cushioned by love, some children will
ignore it, some will sense there are great things beyond
them to be reached for later, some may wonder and ask
questions to be answered wisely, and some may understand
because they are ready. Jesus was only twelve when he
astonished the authorities at the Temple. Moreover, many
children actually witness scenes of violence in films, without meaning or purpose. If we are too prim to mention
life's blood in church, how will the next generation know
there is a difference between violence and sacrifice?

The first time I heard the word "maundy" was long after I had become a member of the church, when I happened to notice it on a large ancient brass plate while visiting a parish church in England. "For giving alms to the poor, the day before Good Friday," explained the sexton. "Jesus commanded it, you know, after he washed the disciples' feet." I was curious about that "maundy," for words are symbols that carry a lot of history in their fiber. I learned that "maunde" is the Middle English word for "command" and though most Christians do not take the washing of each other's feet as a literal order, we serve by doing something more than routine at this time of year about our responsibility to the poor.

Here in Port Jervis we celebrate the story to help us realize our absolute need for the love of Christ. It is part of our preparation for Good Friday and Easter and the One Great Hour of Sharing, dedicated to special needs around the world. We have a covered-dish supper by candlelight at tables placed in the form of a cross and celebrate Holy Communion there at the end of the meal after singing a hymn. This year it was "Let Us Break Bread Together." Members of the choir leave the table first, and take their places on the stairway leading to the sanctuary. As the other people make their way up to participate in the Service of Shadows, or "Tenebrae," we sing. This year it was "Into the Woods My Master Went." It is a holy revealing moment. We are pilgrims together, some vigorous, some feeble, but all thoughtful and none more so than the youth of the Confirmation Class. Once in the church, we are in darkness except for the Christ candle on the Communion table and the seven smaller candles representing the seven shadows:

the Shadow of Betrayal

the Shadow of Inner Agony

the Shadow of Loneliness

the Shadow of Desertion

the Shadow of Accusation

the Shadow of Mockery

the Shadow of Death

After an elder reads the Scripture that relates to each of the candles and then puts it out, the minister says the "Kyrie" and the congregation repeats it after him. When the seventh Scripture has been read, the minister says, "It is finished," and puts out the center candle. We are in darkness. One of the boys in the Orff group then slowly strikes the metalaphone thirty-three times. In the past, the Christ candle has not been lighted again until Chrstmas, but this year it seemed a long time to wait, and it was lighted on Easter morning.

For two years the Ministerial Association in Port Jervis presented an original Passion Play in modern dress to share the meaning of Good Friday with the community. It was held in Orange Square, and the City Hall cooperated by stopping traffic for an hour in that area. The narrator kept it informal so that some of the action could be improvised. Jesus wore jeans and loafers, and John the Baptist carried a guitar. Adults and young people from various churches took part. An informal choir of children and adults sat near the curb, ready to welcome Jesus when he would enter Port Jervis walking along Broome Street.

Some came early and sat in the folding chairs placed here and there about the park, latecomers sat on the edge of the fountain or the grass, or watched from the sidewalk across the street. I think most of them will not soon forget the baptism of Jesus at the fountain by the far-out prophet, or

Jesus' choosing of the disciples as he walked thoughtfully among the crowd, touching this one and that one, until there were eleven. Who will be the twelfth? Who is Judas? Each person has to decide that for himself.

The Presbyterian Church with its classic white pillars and broad steps, facing the square, provided the stage for the final scenes of Jesus' Passion. Although done in panto-mime, it was all too real, and when it was "finished" and the choir sang "Were You There?" we were very still. We had been there.

> Forgive us, Lord, our share
> in this wicked wrong.
> Help us now, before too late,
> to sing your kind of song.

Finally, one of the ministers announced where the Resur-rection would be celebrated on Easter morning at dawn. The singers broke up and the children ran back to the church to meet their parents. They were overjoyed to see Jesus there ahead of them, went close to touch him, took his hand, and did not want to leave with their parents.

A year or so after this Passion Play, our own young people, with the help of a few friends in their school classes, presented *Jesus Christ, Superstar* in our church. It raised some theological questions among us, but because the simplicity of the production carried with it a spirit of Christian humility, several of our people decided not to attend a professional performance later when they had the opportunity. They preferred to remember it as they had seen it at the church.

For weeks before Easter this year, the main thrust of craft activity at our church was making stoles to wear to celebrate the Resurrection. Not for leaders only, but for everyone who might be present at the service. This meant mass production, and all free souls were urged to help. Quite a few did—children, grownups, youth. The stoles

were strips of white felt cut five inches wide and
about two yards long to be decorated as each person saw
fit, with one exception. Because one of our favorite Easter
songs begins with the words, "He's alive and I'm so glad
about it," every stole was to proclaim "He's Alive" in
colored felt letters, but we would chose our own colors
and design our own letters. Beyond that, each person
could be as original as he wished within the context of
Easter.

We made our own stoles first and then spent as much
time as we could making extras for other members and
guests. As they were finished, they were hung side by side
over the large room-dividers in the chapel where their
imaginative variety and colors formed a new kind of art
show in our midst. People stopped to look: "Who made
this one?" "who made that?" Shades of green from emer-
ald to jade, purple, yellow, blue and scarlet, shocking pink
and even brown, cut in patterns plain and fancy. There
were flowers, trees, birds, and suns and moons and stars.
After the "He's Alive" one boy had put "There He
Goes!" One of the adults had designed a vine, one half
bearing fruit, the other dead, to remind us of the life that
abides in Christ and the life that does not. Another used
an Indian thunderbird because to the Christian Indian it
has become a symbol for Christ.

At eleven o'clock on Easter morning, the minister, the
choir director, and the choir entered the church wearing
their stoles, as did every other member of the congregation.
I had completed my own stole early that morning, but had
not imagined how beautiful we would be, all assembled in
our newness. Like grace itself, it had to be experienced to
be understood. The minister spoke of the stoles as our
"burden of joy."

As we sang the Easter hymn based on fourteenth-
century Latin, "Jesus Christ Is Risen Today," a group of
Junior Highs, wearing their stoles, walked in the aisles with

firm, measured step until the "Alleluias." Then they danced for joy. All the way through the hymn there was majesty followed by joy.

Then the Youth Choir gathered around the Communion table with a silver chalice in the center and sang the Australian folksong "Mary, No Need to Cry." It was like an answer to Mary's sorrow on Passion Sunday when Jesus was taken down from the cross in her presence. That day the congregation had sung, "O Sacred Head Now Wounded," and now the teenagers were offering assurance.

Because Pentecost is the brthday of the Christian Church, we celebrate it as a festival even as Christmas and Easter. The minister wears a special robe of red and gold lined with scarlet, and brocaded in a pattern that resembles tongues of fire. The members of the congregation wear something red too, if only a scarf or ribbon, the flowers at the chancel are red and yellow, and of course the red choir curtain is put up to honor the Holy Spirit. One year a brithday cake with lighted candles was carried down the aisle to a table at the front where Dan Rather, our oldest member, joined one of the youngest members to blow out the candles as the congregation prepared to make a silent wish but burst into laughter instead because the candles stubbornly refused to go out.

It has become a tradition that Pentecost is the day our Confirmation Class takes Communion for the first time. They are not only "examined" by the Elders at a special meeting, but also by any who wish to come and ask them questions before the regular service of worship on Pentecost. It is quite something to stand up to this kind of inquiry and they respond with dignity. This year just before taking the bread and the cup, they gathered around the table with the minister in a fellowship toast as we all sang together:

Taste the new wine,
A heady wine, a new brew
our gracious host has here for you and me.
A new product of fermentation,
To make our time on earth a celebration.

Taste the new wine,
Lift high a toast
to the kingly host,
the maker of new wine.[8]

From the Wind River Indian Reservation in Wyoming comes the good news that children there also sing to celebrate. They even take part in the mass celebrated by Father Lew O'Neil, S.J. in St. Stephens, the headquarters mission church, often singing this lovely Indian hymn:

Hey neh ne yah nah
  Hey neh ne hay nah
Hey neh ne yah nah
  Hey nah ne no; hey yah ne no.

I walk in beauty, yes I do, yes I do;
  I talk in beauty, yes I do, yes I do;
I sing in beauty, just for you and only you;
  Hey yah, hey yah ne no.

I yearn for beauty, yes I do, yes I do;
  I learn of beauty, yes I do, yes I do;
I'll beam with beauty, just for you and only you,
  Hey yah, hey yah ne no.[9]

[8] © 1971, Richard K. Avery and Donald S. Marsh. "Taste the New Wine" in *Alive and Singing*. Used by permission.
[9] From *Rendezvous* (July/August 1972), St. Stephens Mission, Wind River Indian Reservation, Wyoming. Used by permission.

These children have much to inspire their singing. They have "sweet bird sounds at dawn, and the pleasant chatter of the Little Wind River in the stillness of the forest . . . the insistent rhythm of the pow-wow drums . . . the ancient chanting of the religious hymns of the Sun Dance." [10]

And they have much to celebrate, for the white missionaries have learned to walk in the other's moccasins, and there are Indian members on the mission staff. I understand that on their part, the Shoshone and Arapaho children know how to share too, that it is part of their heritage.

[10] *Ibid.*

5

Making Up Your Own
Music

C H I L D R E N can make up songs of their own when
conditions are favorable. In the first chapter I shared some
experiences that indicated how much a part of life music
actually is, how meaningful and joyous a part. When we
once realize that the capacity to participate in music lies,
like the Kingdom, within each of us, we want to give opportunities to children to enjoy it and appreciate it. But
we may stop short of believing that children can also have
a part in creating music. If so, it will be a pleasant surprise
to learn that in the collection of songs[1] for grades 1
through 6 in the United Church of Christ curriculum
there are two songs authored and composed by children,
one by a girl of twelve, the other by several children and
youth with their teacher. These both represent exceptional
achievement and we are aware that fulfillment for most
teachers and children in the church will be more humble,
but it can be nonetheless joyful. To be a member of a
group creating a song and then singing it together, no
matter how simple, is in itself a celebration of life.

[1] Max B. Miller and Louise C. Drew, eds., *Sing of Life and Faith*
(Philadelphia: United Church Press, 1969).

When an adult tries painting a picture for the first time he takes a leap into the unfamiliar. So with composing music. Perhaps it is less awesome to call it "making up music" and leave the word "composing" to the professionals. For those who have never tried it but would like to, it is good to be assured that it is great fun, and then if possible, sign up for a workshop if one is available. If not, practice with a group of co-workers or even alone before trying it in a class.

Of course, if you have children at home, that is the best place of all to try it out. You have a group ready-made to respond to each other's ideas and to sing-along with, if and when a song is born. My first attempts at making up a song occurred while I was living for a while under the same roof with my small nieces and nephew. When we got "sick 'n tired" of Old King Cole and his merry old soul, we came up with a song about the day he had a tantrum. When the air was filled with questions, a new song cooperated by opening with these words: "I often wonder why things are and how they got that way."

The learning situation in a modern church Kindergarten group compares favorably with that in an understanding home. There is freedom to move around, there are creative things to do, and guidance when it is needed. If from time to time children can listen to a recording, try out simple rhythm instruments, play singing games and do rhythm exercises, and of course sing, then making up a song eventually will not be an impossible dream. All these activities do not have to take place every Sunday, although I think singing should. As for creating a song, it should not be forced, and will not be, if music is a normal part of the time together. Enthusiasm for music on the part of the teacher is more important than having technical skill, and it is said that except for those with some physical disability of the voice, everyone can learn to sing.

Just how simple and natural creative music can be is illustrated by a true story: a visitor in a kindergarten one Sunday morning arrived in time to hear a little girl share with the other children a song she had made up a few minutes earlier while playing happily in the housekeeping corner. Her teacher had dropped in for "conversation" and shortly after, the song was born: "Thank you, God, for this wonderful gift. Thank you, God, for this wonderful gift."

Unfortunately, in many churches the pressure on the staff to meet routine demands is such that to plan for creative music among older children may seem like an impossible fringe benefit. In my own experience the first breakthrough came when I was working in a Junior Department part time and had more freedom for experiments. We had been having an especially good experience with the parable of the Lost Sheep. The plight of the sheep and the concern of the shepherd had become so vivid and meaningful that one of the classes decided to say something about it in music. It turned out to be "program music" for the piano instead of a song.

We gathered around the piano and blocked out the sequence in words first (their own spelling):

Sheep bouncing	Bramble bush
Nibbling grass	Crying
Shepherd's Call	Shepherd serching
Counting by tens (Shepherd)	Hears cry
Lost sheep goes over hill	Finding!

For the title they chose simply "Sheep Music." The first movement was mostly staccato: "We'll label it 'sheep bouncing,'" they explained. The word "gamboling" was suggested as being somewhat more appropriate, but was rejected out of hand. "Kids would think it was dice instead

of sheep." Agreed. We then moved on to the shepherd's
call and it was unanimous that this should be marked
"Strong." Then the bramble bush? "Slower!" The crying?
"Sad slow." No problem.

To get the actual music off the ground, they left their
chairs and stood as close to the keyboard as possible, and
when anyone had an idea of what the notes should be, he
(or she) picked them out on the keys with one stiff finger.
There were a few trials and disagreements and it took the
entire class period, but as consensus was reached for each
"episode," I jotted the notes down on paper, and when
the parable was completed, played it over for them all in
one piece. We added a few notes here and there for
harmony and tried it through again, quite pleased with it.

But there was still more to come. The organist, who
had got wind of the adventure, arranged their music for
the organ as a surprise, so that the next week when it came
time for the offertory in Junior worship, there were the
sheep bouncing, and there was the little fellow getting lost
and being found. Wow!

I hope no one is mumbling, "That could never happen
to me," because it might, or something even better for your
own situation, especially if one refuses to compare and
complain but will rejoice and expect instead. This same
thing never happened in my own experience again, but a
few songs have, and I think making up a song offers children even more than instrumental music, because it involves
them as both maker and instrument.

The following summer I was with these same children
in a vacation school and we did create music together again,
but this time it was a song. We based it on our theme, "The
Road of the Loving Heart," inspired by the friendship
that grew up between the native people of Samoa and
Robert Louis Stevenson who had had to go there for his
health. We had become interested in him because there was

a stone fragment in the sanctuary which had come as a gift from St. Giles Cathedral in Edinburgh, Stevenson's home city. We made a collage about various other people who had walked that road and then we were moved to try a song. It began with the words, "Jesus started the road of the loving heart, and he called the disciples along the way. . . ." At that point names of the original disciples were called out one by one in a speaking voice. The second verse was about others who follow the way of Jesus and at the end of that the names of *modern* disciples were spoken as before, one by one, by members of the group. The last words were an invitation to join:

> We can walk that same road too,
> You and I—and you and you.

One way to stimulate a sense of rhythm is for children to note the rhythm of their own play or those around them as they walk, run, swing, jump rope, or go down a slide with a swish-boom! At home they can watch mother mixing a cake, sweeping, ironing—if she still does! Or father pounding a nail, mowing the lawn, or sawing a board. An adult can improve her own sense of rhythm in this way too, adding waves at the beach or wind in the trees for drama, the sunrise and the setting of the sun for majesty.

Recently our Adult Choir sang a three-part canon by Natalie Sleeth, and for a week afterward these words kept singing in my mind:

> Praise Him, praise Him
> Praise the Lord forever
> Come and praise Him,
> Come and praise the Lord.[2]

[2] Natalie Sleeth, "A Canon of Praise," © 1969 Choristers Guild in Choristers Guild Letters. Used by permission.

They have a strong beat and it would be great fun as a rhythm experience for Primary groups to sing in unison while pantomiming the rhythmic motion of ringing bells in a steeple. The rope used for a large bell is quite thick, and the bell-ringer grasps it with both hands above his head and gives it a long, hard pull. If anyone tries it, let the children know that the original reason for having bells in a church steeple was to ring out the good news of God's love. It calls people to come to the church and celebrate.

For preschool children a good bell song for rhythm is "Sing a Song of Church Bells" in *Songs for Early Childhood*.[3] Children enjoy listening to the music first, because it is a good imitation of bells, and to start the exercise the teacher can sing and the children concentrate on ringing the bells. Later they can do both. Perhaps still later, they will make up a bell tune of their own.

Still another way to sharpen your own "rhythm readiness" is to read poems out loud that have a definite beat. Relax and enjoy the lilt and movement. Clap the rhythm, tap it with a pencil or with your feet, wave an arm or two, skip a little, hop a little, jump. This will help free you to lead the children later.

If you do not have poems at home, there are anthologies in the library that include both old and new favorites. I have mentioned a few in the bibliography at the end of this book. And don't forget poems that are just for fun, like "Godfrey Gorden Gustavus Gore," [4] the boy who would never shut a door. Or "Antonio, Antonio, who was tired of living alonio." [5] It is good to laugh in church as well as in other places.

[3] Philadelphia: Westminster Press, 1958.
[4] Isabel J. Peterson, ed., *The First Book of Poetry* (New York: Franklin Watts, 1954).
[5] *Ibid.*

In some school systems, poetry reading and writing are more important than in others, so that the readiness of children to make up words for a song in a church class will vary. One hears now and then of schools that have made poetry as exciting as stickball through the efforts of imaginative teachers such as Kenneth Koch at P.S. 61 in New York City. In England, a Children's Poetry Festival is held each year in June at the Playhouse in Nottingham, where children of different ages come from other schools in the area to read their own poems. In 1973 there were over eight hundred entries, and from the interest shown, it can be said that poetry will draw a crowd as well as cricket. One school has even brought out its own anthology of poetry.

Most children know at least a few nursery rhymes from memory, and you can always begin with these in preschool or early Primary fun-time. Say them together and clap out the rhythm as you did when you practiced by yourself. You can add a drum or rhythm sticks, but it may be better not to use an instrument with a tone until after you have your own melody. Try it and see which works best for you.

An easy nursery rhyme to experiment with is "Tom, Tom, the piper's son, stole a pig and away he run." It is short, the rhythm is strong and simple. Don't worry about the grammar, it's a fun rhyme. Just clap the rhythm, slowly first, then faster for variety. Now try sustaining the sound of each word as you say it slowly, and almost before you know it, your voice is singing instead of speaking. If you draw out the word "Tom-m-" and close your lips, you have a hum. If you say the rhyme through, staying on the one tone, you have a chant. Next, try improvising a tune yourself, just for the first line, and leave it in the air for one of the children to finish. Perhaps one of them will! There is no telling until you try.

Instead of putting a tune to the words of a poem already made, as above, it is possible to put new words to an old tune. Margaret Adams, a friend, tells how she did this recently. In writing a summer curriculum, she needed a song about the joy of worshiping God. She took her autoharp to the room for three- and four-year-olds one Sunday morning and played through the first half of Beethoven's "Hymn to Joy." Then using "Alleluia's" for the first two measures of each stanza, she asked the children to help her complete sentences for each. Here are the lines they made together:

> Alleluia, alleluia, children bring their songs of joy.
> Alleluia, alleluia, so sing every girl and boy.
> Alleluia, alleluia, thanks to God the people say,
> Alleluia, alleluia, He is with us every day.

When we had an ecology day at the Port Jervis church, I put new words to the old tune "Twinkle Twinkle Little Star" for the Nursery-Kindergarten class but without involving the children in the authorship. My main purpose was to have a singing game they could enjoy at the same time they were learning how to help take care of the environment:

> Litter, litter, thick or thin,
> Pick it up and drop it in,
> Pick it up and drop it in
> To a basket or a bin.
>
> Litter, litter, we will win,
> Pick it up and drop it in.

For the game, we put a large wastebasket in the middle of the floor, circled around it singing the song until we were sure of it, then pantomimed the picking up and the dropping in. The song and the game caught on, and that afternoon when all ages went out as teams on a litter-hunt, some in the park, others along the streets, I like to think that even the preschool children who could not all go understood. One of the five-year-olds in my neighborhood came home from the class, gathered a group of friends and picked up the litter around our own buildings, sometimes, alas! with self-righteous indignation: "How come they don't know any better? Stupid!" (Where could they have picked up that spiritual litter?)

Some times under the strain of trying to make rhymes, the lines get stiff and artificial. It may be a relief to children to know that songs don't have to rhyme any more than poems do. You can choose. The poems quoted below illustrate the point. One of them rhymes, two do not. All three were read at the Children's Poetry Festival in 1970.[6] The first one has seven verses, of which three are quoted below:

COLORS

I wonder what green is like?
It is fresh, it is crisp,
It is the grass, it is the leaves,
It means Springtime.

I wonder what brown can be like?
It is dull, it is deep,
It is the chestnut,
It means Autumn.

I know what black is like.
It is dark, it is empty,
It is death, it is grief,
It means blindness.

Moira Delsaer, at age twelve

[6] Permission to quote their verses has been granted by the three poets.

Those lines do not rhyme but they have rhythm and creative thoughts that could be sung if they had a tune and the poet wished it. Poems don't have to be sung, and neither songs nor poems have to rhyme.

On the other hand, for some children the rhymes are great fun, and I can imagine that the boy who wrote the next poem enjoyed finding words that would kindle a spark by sounding alike, especially the punch lines in the last verse:

HAIR

Hair long,
Hair short,
Hair rough,
of any sort.

Hair light,
Hair dark,
Hair bright,
like a spark.

Hair silver,
Hair gold,
Thick when young,
but thin when old.

William Minnitt, at age ten

The third poem is the shortest and by the youngest:

WHALES

Whales are over eighty feet
They would not be able to
go through the garden gate
and they never have to wash themselves.

Catherine Goodwin at age eight

Anyone wanting to make up a tune for that delightful comment would have to be very careful to keep it simple enough to let the idea shine through. If a poem is a song waiting for a tune, it is a sensitive matter to find the right one. When tunes get too fancy, meanings are covered up and would be better off spoken, not sung. This has been a source of conflict in church music through the ages. But in all kinds of songs, the best tunes are those that match the words in spirit. Perhaps this is one reason why plainsong appears again and again in church music like a plumbline to remind the musicians not to steal the scene. This is why folktunes appear more often in church hymnals than they did, and why families and communal groups like to sing them together.

In their two collections of songs for children,[7] the Society of Brothers includes folksongs gathered from many countries over a period of about forty years. Incidentally, most of them rhyme, but some of them do not. Also included are a number of original songs by different members of the community. The word ideas for "My Little Sister" in *Sing Through the Seasons* were contributed by a four-year-old child, and the tune, although by an adult, matches the ideas in childlike simplicity. Several other songs were composed by the preschool and kindergarten groups, two of them in honor of a new baby: "Tiny Little Baby" and "Little Brother in the Cradle." The word ideas for the first were given by four children of the same family, and the tune is by a fifth child. The words and music for the second are by a seven-year-old boy for his new brother. Both are brimful of gentle love, and "Tiny Little Baby" [8] has humor.

[7] Society of Brothers, eds., *Sing Through the Day* (1968) and *Sing Through the Seasons* (1972) (Rifton, N.Y.: Plough Publishing House).
[8] Used by permission.

Tiny little baby, we love you very much,
Your soft fuzzy hair we would like to touch.
I get a surprise when you open your eyes;
they are so big and shiny.

Your little pink feet are so wiggly and sweet
Your green socks are so big they fall off.

The word "off" at the end of that line is given a whole
note, as though the children must pause to chuckle fondly
at the happening. Then the song concludes:

Tiny little baby, we love you very much,
We'll rock you and we'll sing to you
until you go to sleep.

The Society of Brothers is the American transplant, so
to speak, of the German Bruderhof, a group dedicated to
living out the teachings of Jesus in a brotherhood having
"all things in common" as recorded in the Acts of the
Apostles. Dissolved by the Nazi regime, they found their
way eventually to the United States where they have
established three communities: the original one at Rifton,
New York, where they operate the Plough Publishing
House and make creative toys for children, another at
Norfolk, Connecticut, and the third at Farmington, Pennsylvania. There is a fourth in Sussex, England.

Commenting on the love of music in the Society of
Brothers, Marlys Swinger, herself a member who is involved with both composing and arranging music, says it
has grown out of their life together. The children actually
sing together from the time they are one or two years old
and do rhythm instruments in the kindergarten and preschool groups, but it is all a joyous "fun-time" together,
rather than specific step-by-step planning. Sometimes children spend some quiet time at the piano and discover a

little "melody" of four or five notes which they find pleasing. Or when they are anticipating the Christmas season, or when one of the children has a new baby in the family, the teacher or some other older person may sit down with the children and say, "Let's make a song." And the ideas come forth, all the things the children would like to sing about.

For the concept of music education developed by Zoltan Kodaly, a simple scale of five tones (do-re-mi-sol-la)[9] is recommended for children until they are eight or in the fourth grade. After that, the usual seven-tone scale (do-re-mi-fa-sol-la-ti)[10] may not be too difficult. The five-tone scale is the same as the other except that the two half-tones *fa* and *ti* are omitted. This could be a helpful guideline for anyone experimenting with younger children in creating original music. (Many native folktunes use the five-tone scale. Kodaly believed them to be a precious heritage for every country, to be learned and treasured by each succeeding generation. In the context of the church we have the spirituals and some of the psalms set to music.)

Psalms are often used in creative music with children. In the case of younger children, one can start the search for a tune with a single line, such as the beginning of Psalm 138:

I thank you, Lord, with all my heart.

Instead of giving the children a single note and asking them to add another, it is best to improvise the first half with a melody of your own and let them finish it. Melody flows. In this case, the teacher would improvise "I thank you, Lord," and the children would improvise "with all my heart." Several children might want to try it, and of

[9] Pentatonic scale.
[10] Diatonic scale.

course each one is respected. The entire group can sing
the phrase together and then the entire line. This can be
the beginning of responsive or antiphonal singing for
them. A little thank-you song like this could be used by
the class in many ways, as a grace, a special prayer on
someone's birthday, or a spontaneous burst of joy. Primary
departments have long used a song of this type based on
Psalm 104, as mentioned in the third chapter:

> I will sing to the Lord as long as I live.

If the teacher is alert to lead off with songs like these,
when something special happens unexpectedly, the children themselves will come to think of them as a musical
comment, an "Amen" with a tune, another way of saying,
"Wow!"

For older children, Psalm 117 would be a good one to
work with. The entire psalm is only five lines long, the
shortest one in the psalter:

> Praise the Lord, all nations!
>   Praise Him, all peoples!
> His constant love for us is strong,
> And His faithfulness is eternal.
> Praise the Lord!

This could become a prayer song for World Communion
Day, World Day of Prayer, or One Great Hour of Sharing, and with it could be sung songs of other countries
such as those in *The Whole World Singing* by Edith
Lovell Thomas, or *Sing, Children, Sing* sponsored by the
United States Committee of UNICEF, or *Sing Through
the Seasons* mentioned above.

[11] *Songs and Hymns for Primary Worship* (Philadelphia: Westminster
Press, 1963).

An unusual arrangement involving primary children with the psalms both spoken and sung was worked out by Jeanette Perkins Brown when she was on the staff at Riverside Church, New York City. She chose lines from three psalms for the framework, the children gave their own ideas about the goodness of God, and she phrased them in four paragraphs with the singing response after each. The ideas given by the children are summarized here for brevity. It is my understanding that they worked out the music for the response together, and chose to call the liturgy "Our Psalm." [12]

Our Psalm

Sing a new song to the Lord;
He has done wonderful things! (Ps. 98:1)
Give thanks to the Lord, because he is good.
(Ps. 106:1)

He fills the world with beauty to enjoy
    (golden stars, rainbows in the sky, trees . . .
    little colored flowers in the grass).

    Sing to Him, sing praise to Him;
    tell all the wonderful things He has done!
    (Ps. 105:2)
He has put beautiful thoughts into the minds of men
    (so they can paint pictures, build churches with
    windows full of color . . . carve angel figures. . . .

    Sing to Him, sing praise to Him;
    tell all the wonderful things He has done!

---

[12] Used by permission of the J. P. Brown estate. Mrs. Brown used the King James Version of the Psalms in her text. The quotations here are from Today's English version.

He has given us minds to discover the wonders
(electricity . . . ships . . . planes. . .).

Sing to Him, sing praise to Him;
tell all the wonderful things He has done!

He has put love into the world
(Children have homes, food, care . . . and can be
helpers to make all people safe and happy).

Sing to Him, sing praise to Him;
tell all the wonderful things He has done!

Using this as a guide, any group can choose favorite
psalm lines to create a liturgy for worship.

If teachers feel the urge to make up songs themselves,
why not? It can strengthen their own "being force" as
they try to help the children become more creative, besides
being fun for its own sake. When the church school here
had a UNICEF party on Hallowe'en, one group made a
large picture of the world to go on the bulletin board, another, gaily colored figures of chidren to circle it, while I
made up a song, *both* words and music this time, about
helping to carry your neighbor's load:

We're not very big
but we're not too small
to hold out a hand
and make a friendly call.

If your neighbor's load is heavy
You can lift a little bit
even if you can not
carry all of it.

So . . . lift up the load,
hold out your hand,
be a friendly friend,
try to understand.

We printed the words with a black Magic Marker on
bright orange paper in honor of Hallowe'en and put them
in plain sight for those to read who could. First we sat on
the floor with the world and the children and the song in
our midst and talked about how much the world needs
love, both in feeling and in practical packages like shoes
and food and clothes and medicine and money to buy
these. Then we learned the song and worked out gestures,
a lively send-off before the children went off with their
decorated cartons for Trick or Treat for UNICEF.

Interestingly enough, the song was useful again only a
few days later when, as a visiting witch in a mask from
Woolworth's, I taught it to the children at the library
story hour.

There are any number of stories in both the Old and
New Testaments that lend themselves to original songs.
They happen best out of doing other things related to the
story. In another chapter I mentioned how we sang "Go
Down Moses" with an autoharp during the study of
Egypt. After that I tried an original song on the plagues,
a subject popular with children and in folk art. Behind
the altar of an old church in Bavaria is a quaint series
of paintings on wood showing every one of the ten
plagues in dramatic detail, one plague to a square. The
Primary children had made their own drawings of the
plagues, the most vivid one being a hand covered with
boils, which was pinned along with other plagues to the
banks of the Nile in a mural. We had hoped everyone
could mold a frog in green plasticene, but time was short
and we moved on to the song. In attempting creative

music, whether alone or with children, it helps to narrow the interest to one particular incident or situation. Just as the artist painted only one plague at a time on each of his wooden squares, the song was about only one plague, the frogs. It was a funny song, with the frogs poking fun at Egypt, and although the children did not take part directly in composing it, they were hilariously involved with leaping and jumping when they sang it.

While helping one year with after-school activities related to the Youth Choir, it was my privilege to try another song, this time from the New Testament. It was to be about Jesus, but there are so many stories about him, which one would it be? Finally the choice settled on Zacchaeus, the little swindler, and how Jesus came into his life. Don Marsh worked with the children in art and drama, and then we put the three efforts together. There were sketches of Zacchaeus' neighborhood in modern terms like "Pete's Fishnet Repair Shop," "Good Samaritan Motel," "Martha's Pizza Palace." The song began like this:

> Zacchaeus was a little man
> when Jesus came that way
> and so he climbed into a tree
> to see if he could see

> that Jesus man, that Jesus man
> he'd heard so much about
> and why he was so special
> he wanted to find out.

The song began with Zacchaeus climbing the tree so he could see Jesus, and the drama naturally began there too. Remembering how Thornton Wilder had used a stepladder in *Our Town*, I would probably have hunted for one to represent a tree, but Don's idea was much more creative. The tallest boy was the tree from which Zacchaeus had his first glimpse of Jesus!

It was some time later that the Youth Choir gave me what was probably the greatest surprise of my life: they sang "That Jesus Man" for their special number during Sunday morning worship, with piano and Orff instruments. They had kept the secret well, posting a sentry at the door of the church during their rehearsal before service in case I happened to come that way. Vive le Youth Choir, the choirmaster, Zacchaeus, and that Jesus Man!

The summer that we had a country day-camp with two other churches in Port Jervis, the most popular story was the one about Bartimaeus, the blind man who was healed by Jesus. After hearing it, the children took a "blind walk" down the woods road, keeping their eyes closed and holding each other by the hand. They agreed not to talk so that they could hear what was going on around them.

Back at camp, they sketched pictures of what they had "seen with their ears." Birds, a squirrel, a car, crickets, leaves rustling in the wind, feet walking, and so on.

With this little store of empathy for the blind, they painted pictures of the miracle of healing as each interpreted it, and then fastened them on the trees in the open grove, their outdoor gallery. But this was not enough. They also acted out the story, taking turns being Jesus and Bartimaeus or one of the disciples following along.

The song itself we did after camp one day back at the church where there was a piano. The creative idea for it was that the blind man spent much time begging for money until Jesus came along, and then what he wanted most was to see.

The very thought of making up a song inspired one of the black boys to do a joyous impromtu dance, after which we got down to business on the song. It began:

> Bartimaeus was a blind man
> on the road to Jericho

and ended

> Jesus healed him,
> gave him vision
> "Praise the Lord
> Now I can see!"

Even this was not the end of the story's creative influence. The next fall the song was used in church school as the keynote of a worship service which was an experiment in multi-media. We used some of the Bartimaeus paintings made at camp, some made previously relating to the mirace of Jesus stilling the storm and his calling of the disciples. We used colored slides of others, and copies of paintings by well-known artists relating either to the disciples or to the two miracles, and we used a recording of the storm movement of Beethoven's Sixth Symphony. The words of the song were posted in the center of the display and were sung by the group antiphonally. The song went well, especially the second time through when everybody shouted "Praise the Lord" instead of singing it.

PRAISE THE LORD!

It has been said that songs with creative ideas and singable rhythm can stimulate new original songs in the unconscious minds of people who hear them. I am beginning to think this may be so. Until I came to Port Jervis, where we continually sing songs that fit that description, it had been years since I had made up a song. Lack of time is part of the explanation but I doubt if it is all of it. Whatever the reason, it was exciting to wake up one morning with these words flowing free:

It's a singing world
it's a brand new day
the sun is shining all the way.

and to add more words before lunch, to make a poem:

Gone the terror,
gone the dread,
we are risen from the dead!

Life's so easy with a song
seems at first there's something wrong,
but you see things clear
when you lose your fear—

The music you hear
is the song the world will sing
when the whole world learns to sing
when the whole world learns
to sing a new day song.

It was much later, however, that I worked out a tune to
fit the words and it came with something of a struggle, not
in a single burst like those first three lines. Like life itself,
not complete in the first three steps, and it will take the
rest of my life and beyond to sing it as it is meant to be.

A letter from the teacher mentioned at the beginning of
this chapter gives interesting answers to the questions I
asked on discovering the song she and her group had written. Here are some of them, shared with her permission.

The teacher is Doreen Newport (known as "Bunty")
of the Emmanuel United Reformed Church in Cambridge,
England, and those involved in the song group were eight
11- to 13-year-olds of the Intermediate Department of the
"Children's Church." They had been thinking how dread-
ful the world would be without the beauty of nature, the
arts, science, and people, and one Sunday morning put

their ideas into words for a song. The meaning advances in
depth with each stanza, concluding with the last three
quoted below:

6   Think of a world without any people
     Think of a street with no one living there
     Think of a town without any houses
     No one to love and nobody to care.

     We thank Thee, Lord, for families and friendships
     We thank Thee, Lord, and praise Thy holy name.

7   Think of a world without any worship
     Think of a world without His only son
     Think of a cross without resurrection
     Only a grave and not a victory won.

     We thank Thee, Lord, for showing us our Savior
     We thank Thee, Lord, and praise Thy holy name.

8   Thanks to our Lord for being here among us
     Thanks be to Thee for sharing all we do
     Thanks for our church and all the love we find here
     Thanks for the place and all its promise true.

     We thank Thee, Lord, for life in all its richness
     We thank Thee, Lord, and praise Thy holy name.[13]

That same afternoon Doreen Newport invited any who
wanted to help make up the tune to come to her home and
carry on the good work. About six showed up and "had a
go," emerging fairly quickly with the melody and refrain.
She added guitar chords and a simple guitarlike accompaniment for piano if no guitars were available. At its first
performance at a Festival Service in May 1966, it was done

---

[13] From "Think of a World," written and composed jointly by children of the Intermediate Department of the Emmanuel United Reformed Church in Cambridge, England. Arranged by their teacher
Doreen Newport and Peter Cutts. Copyright © 1969 by Galliard Ltd.
All rights reserved. Used by permission.

with three guitars played by undergraduates from the student Congregational Society who regard Emmanuel as their spiritual home during term.

Since then, a different type of accompaniment has been put to it for use in churches where only an organ is available. This is the one which appears in the American publication, although Mrs. Newport still conceives it as a "folksy piece," if not jazzy, which would be good with double-bass and percussion. It has been performed in a variety of ways on television, especially from churches in Scotland because of the interest in new music and new words at the ecumenical center in Dunblane called "Scottish Churches House." It was in their publication *Dunblane Praises No. 1* that "Think of a World" first circulated.

From the Cameroon in Africa comes word that original music flourishes in the Church there. On furlough recently from the Presbyterian mission among the people of the Bassa tribe, Marabelle Taylor played a tape which I had the privilege of hearing. She had recorded the worship service of their "Choir Sunday" when three choirs of all ages, two of women's voices, one of men's, sang a Bassa liturgy entirely of their own original music except for two American hymn tunes for which they had made their own words.

A thousand people attended the event, five hundred sitting inside the church on logs or planks, five hundred outside on the ground. The service began with processional singing, "Rejoice, Rejoice," and dancing in a slow step, then shifted to the congregation, with clapping. The choirmaster led without any accompaniment and the singing was never in unison. Only once, after a break in the singing, the pitch was given by a short phrase from an accordian.

"The Lord is merciful for ever and ever" they sing in rich harmony, then suddenly shift to a new key with different rhythm and tempo continuing with the words: [14]

14 Used by permission.

God the Father is worthy of praise,
Christ the Son is worthy of praise
The Holy Spirit is worthy of praise,
One God is worthy of praise.

Now the pastor speaks, followed by the hymn "How I Love Thy Word" and a pastoral prayer:

Only Thou art merciful,
Only Thou art able to forgive,
Only Thou canst give us life eternal,
Forgive us and make us new,
In Christ's name.

The singing response of the congregation at this point is slow and sustained, without clapping.

The people outside continue to sing with those inside, although it is difficult to keep together during the sustained portions.

We are ashamed before You,
Have mercy upon us and forgive us.

Now the pastor prays:

Accept us with Thy hands,
Only Thou art merciful.

And the people respond by singing the same words, followed by the Apostles' Creed said in unison, from memory. None of the service is printed, neither words nor music, for the people learn by rote easily.

Now the clapping begins again as they sing the joyous words:

Alleluia, Thou art worthy of praise
forever and ever.
The Comforter has come,
the Helper of hearts.
Rejoice, rejoice, rejoice.

In the afternoon the choirs go out to several villages and
sing outdoors. Everybody comes to hear, "everybody who
can waddle." There are several evangelists and much joy,
something like a rock festival in an African setting. Ever
since missionaries began to work *with* the people instead
of *for* them, creative innovations like this have taken place.
The people are free to be themselves, and their relationships with the fraternal workers are open and deep. Sig-
nificantly, the Bassa people have given Marabelle Taylor a
special name in their own language which means "Beautiful Day."

Miss Taylor's first letter home after returning to Africa
from furlough closed with this thought: "So I'm off into
the new year with babies in my arms, strength in my body
for all He gives me to do . . . praise and thanksgiving on
my lips, the sunlight on my way by day and the moon and
stars by night—so many of my nights are active and need
their light."

Beautiful Day and Beautiful Night.

6

The Healing Power of Music

PEOPLE have believed for a very long time in the power of music to heal. The Greeks believed it so fervently that during at least one threat of civil war they held a music contest in the hope of bringing the antagonists together without violence. It worked! To foster their faith in music as a "divine discovery," they created the legend of Orpheus, who played the lyre so beautifully that forest creatures came out of hiding to listen, and wild ones were tamed. His music would even have freed his beloved Euridyce from Hades had he not doubted and booked back. The cost of Orpheus' failure of faith was the loss of his power to make music, which so angered the women of Thrace that they tore him to pieces. The Greeks had a way of making the point of a myth unforgettable.

From the Jucarilla Apache Indians comes a charming legend about the process of creation: when people saw that the sun and moon were too small and dim, the great creator, Black Hactcin, told them they "had better start singing." So they sang together "to make the sun and moon grow larger; and as they sang, the sun and moon began to grow; their light became strong and bright; and the sun and moon moved in their courses just as they do today."

Today there is realistic evidence of cause and effect between singing and human growth. In Hungary, those schools in which Zoltan Kodály succeeded in establishing music as a regular part of the curriculum, with singing every day, have shown marked improvement in the quality of learning in the other disciplines. And Eva Rozgonyi, a graduate of the Liszt Academy in Budapest, told in a recent Kodály workshop in this country of a rewarding experience in teaching a group of somewhat retarded children. At first they stumbled in their singing, but by the end of the year they not only could sing, they could also read music. To help one child understand what an interval is, she lifted the child's arms on a high note, and lowered them on a low note.

A thousand years before Christ, King Saul depended on David and his harp to lift him from the dark moods that beset him. As a boy, David had studied at the school for music founded by Samuel and it may have been there that he learned to sing and play the harp that calmed a king.

Some eight hundred years later, an English monk known as the Venerable Bede, who wrote the first history of England, was an enthusiastic believer in the renewing power of music. "Music is the most worthy, courteous, pleasant, and joyous and lovely of all knowledge. . . . music encourages us to bear the heaviest afflictions, administers consolation in every difficulty, refreshes the broken spirit, removes headache, and cures crossness and melancholy." Perhaps it was music that helped him to triumph over the trials of life in the monastery, for later he was made a saint. I am reminded of the ruins of an abbey in another country where a visitor is shown a stone stair leading from the dormitory to the chapel down which the monks filed to sing the night service. In the annals of the abbey was an account of the rebuke given to one of the monks because he had slapped the abbot. One wonders what worse things might have happened had there been no opportunity to sing.

In the first chapter we considered the intimate relationship between music and one's own true self. An inside-out version of this was shown in the television series "All in the Family" when Archie Bunker came home singing for a change.

"What's wrong?" asked his wife.

"Nothing," he replied, "this is the happiest day of my life. There's a vacancy on the bowling team because a guy dropped dead."

Part of the truth we receive from a song comes from the unity of it. Two things important to each other are knit together: thought and feeling, words and music. If either one is out of tune with the true nature of life, the other is weakened. If both are, the song is false. We speak of prayer as talking to God, but in a deeper awareness of His presence, we say "talking *with* God." We often "sing to the Lord," but I have never heard anyone speak of singing *with* Him. Let's do.

We read in Genesis that the morning stars sang together as they were being created. I think God must have liked that so much that He sang along with them. It is not His nature to be on the sidelines. Today more that ever, we are a singing church and He must like to see that, too, and be singing along. More accurately, we are singing along with Him. It is not a matter of logic, however, but of being aware of reality, in a way that is new to some of us. So new, that even an old song seems new when you know who is singing with you. You don't have to be in the choir. He is singing in the congregation, too. With the person beside you—both sides—those in front of you, behind you, and on the far side of the church. If you don't

carry a tune easily, let the tune carry you. A song can lift
the spirit, renew the mind, and lead one into joy. It may
change our style of living, for when people sing together
in worship, God's love becomes real to them, and new
beginnings are possible. They are for young and old, "the
bald as well as the short and long hairs. . . . Christians and
Pagans and even sinners! . . . To be alive spiritually is to
be able to change, adapt, move, dropout, and start all over
again . . . and again—"[1]

Children may find personal release from emotional stress
through song. "When I'm Feeling Lonely," by Avery and
Marsh, speaks to all people of all ages and is popular with
our Youth Choir. This may surprise adults who forget that
their own youth was not a time of uninterrupted bliss.

> When I'm feeling lonely,
> When I need a friend,
> When I need to know this
> Isn't the end. . . .[2]

It is reassuring to hear psychologists say that singing a
song like that will not freeze a mood of sadness but release
it, and a true story from a church that uses this song will
illustrate the point: Sally had trouble relating to children
of her own age, and often asked for the "lonely" song. If
it was not convenient to include it in the group work, she
would sometimes wander over to the piano during free
time and pick out the tune by herself, then return to the
group, apparently relaxed and content. Life flows more
freely for Sally now. She is taller in several ways and no
longer asks for the "lonely" song. She is also growing
pretty.

[1] From Carlton Young's introduction to *The Genesis Songbook*,
compiled by Young. © 1973, Agape Press, Carol Stream, Ill. Used by
permission.

[2] © 1967, Richard K. Avery and Donald S. Marsh, in *Hymns Hot
and Carols Cool*. Used by permission.

In solitude a child may make up a song of her own to express a depth of feeling she does not know how to share with another, or merely does not wish to. Jennifer, who was only four, did this one day while I was a guest in her home. Her mother was away at work and everyone else had gone out. She was sitting on a table dangling her feet over the edge and looking out the window at the city streets below. She may have forgotten I was still in my room, or perhaps she was so absorbed in a recent experience of loss that she would have felt alone even in a crowd.

Her father had just left for a prolonged stay in Europe and she missed him intensely. Only the year before, a much-loved grandmother who had been taking care of her for two years had flown back to her own home halfway around the world. This then was the second big separation of her life, the second time of desolation.

In a minor key, she began to sing a few startling words over and over like a chant:

I know that I must die,

I know that I must die. . . .

She would pause and then repeat them, pause and repeat them again. As far as I knew there had been no incident of death in either the family or the neighborhood, yet she seemed to be making a connection between the sadness of the temporary separation of her father and the sadness of death. This alone is not too unusual, since young children do not distinguish the difference in time between "forever" and "for a while." But I got the impression that she had somehow caught the idea that death must come to everyone and that this included her and she must learn to accept that fact. I know this may sound like overinterpreting on my part, that four-year-olds can't think abstractly and so on, but I still feel that deep down at that moment Jennifer was some sort of kin to Edna St. Vincent Millay when she wrote the last line of one of her sonnets: "Music my rampart and my only one."

In the Old Testament, when Moses turned to music he put it this way: "The Lord is my strength and my song." We are advised in the Psalms to "come into his presence with singing." Do we really believe that is what happens when we sing? Then what are we waiting for? I doubt that Moses had a great singing voice. He stuttered, but he sang anyway. He saw the burning bush, he talked with God, and walked on holy ground.

If we are out of touch for any reason at any age with our own true selves or others, and long for harmony, music can help us find it. One of my treasured pictures is a clipping of a small boy in a school for the deaf, "hearing" music for the first time in his life. Pressing his cheek against the end of the piano being played by his teacher, he is catching the rhythm through the vibrations in the wood, and on his face is a look of utter rapture.

To see a human being break the barrier of a severe handicap with the help of rhythm perceived in a new way is a

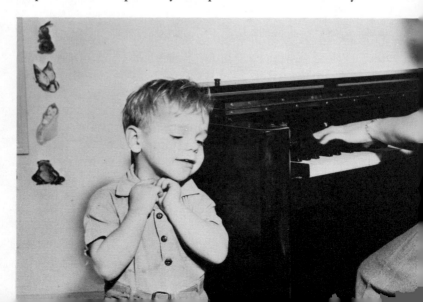

poignant experience. In a documentary film of Helen Keller, there is a scene showing her with Martha Graham and a group of dancers moving to the beat of a drum. Miss Keller feels the vibrations as the dancers whirl around her and abandons herself joyously to the rhythm, swaying and keeping perfect time with her hands. For her, rhythm and being open to it made the difference between being deprived and being enabled to participate in movement.

Striking accounts of the healing power of music are given in *Music Therapy in Special Education* by Paul Nordoff and Clive Robbins, who are therapists of wide experience in the field. There is the story of Edward, an orphan who had lived in several foster homes and was plagued with indecision. The staff at the center where he had been sent for treatment decided to try him in a play that had a cymbal part. It had a demanding rhythm, and during early rehearsals he had to struggle against his lack of confidence. He would raise his arms and begin the downward beat, but arrest the stroke at the very last second. But the leader kept on trying, going over the part again and again, and the child developed a kind of loyalty to trying again too, until finally he was able to follow through, and he became devoted to his musical activity. His regular classroom behavior also became more purposeful.

Then there is Patti, a sweet, passive eight-year-old child who had a singing voice typical of a Mongoloid—low pitched, indistinct, with a range of only one or two tones near middle C. She was given opportunities to play a bell part in the orchestra and later even a violin part in a play. This she greatly enjoyed, holding the violin as if she were one with it. She began to be more lively and alert, developing independence in her school work and even a sense of humor in group relationships. To quote: "Two years later in an assembly, we heard a new singing voice, lovely, warm, true. It was Patti. She was singing in the group with conscious pleasure." They thought it was possible that the clear high D vibration of the violin so close to her had somehow penetrated her mind as well as her body, perhaps unconsciously as well as consciously, giving her a tonal center for her music, and allowing her the confidence she needed to expand her personality in other ways as well.

Finally, there is Gail, the girl who screamed. Both shrewd and intelligent, at seven years she was able to rule her parents. The day she entered the school she screamed in protest on the bus and all day in class. After several days the parents were asked to keep her at home. Later the parents urged the principal to give Gail another chance, and it happened that her return coincided with the arrival of Nordoff and Robbins, who had come to work in music therapy at the school. They heard her scream in her classroom as they were about to begin a music assembly in the auditorium, but knowing her story, they felt that music might be the key to her problem, and so they brought her right into the auditorium, yelling loudly.

Some children were annoyed at Gail's screaming, but the leaders paid no attention to her and the children finally took their cue to do the same. The screams subsided to more normal crying until she stopped and stared at the ceiling. Suddenly she began to sing with the others and her voice was on pitch. At the end of the assembly, she went to the piano and played single tones forcefully with one stiff finger, saying, "I'm helping you." One of the leaders kept her with him in an instrument class as he worked with the other children and she was no problem. She did not cry again that day and never screamed in school again. After a few weeks she even accepted the bus ride as part of going to school.

In the concluding chapter of *Music Therapy in Special Education*, the authors state that music should not be thought of as a static or routine activity, but as an up-building, evolving process. "The work can then be more flexible, giving emphasis on the need for time . . . time for experience to stabilize and deepen, time for their memories to work on their experiences and transform them into understanding and ability. If you work with music therapy in this spirit, time will be on your side." They go on to say that as activities build, children who have not taken part at first will be drawn into them and often surprise you with how much they have learned while watching and listening.

Further, Nordoff and Robbins say that a child with a pathological problem will become isolated in his condition, even identifying himself with his difficulties. Group therapy breaks down this isolation and sometimes even the blocks that have been preventing normal development, through its power to envelop all the children in a single experience and unite their efforts. The arts are helpful in promoting emotional vitality, especially music and drama. The hope, they insist, is to release the child not just for an hour or so each week but permanently. They mention three special things to try to change or at least improve: (1) the child's responsiveness; (2) awareness of self; (3) attitude toward others. To quote the last words in the book, "We in special education share these responsibilities for we are working for the whole future of human beings and for the relationships they will form throughout their lives." [3]

In the Gospel story, Bartimaeus was physically healed of his blindness, but Zacchaeus was spiritually healed of his small stature. He was still a short man after he met Jesus, but transformed inwardly by the renewing of his

[3] Paul Nordhoff and Clive Robbins, *Music Therapy in Special Education.* © The John Day Company (New York, 1971). Used by permission.

mind. In my visit to the New York Institute for the Education of the Blind, I have seen how that gracious place makes this second kind of healing possible.

It was on the occasion of their anniversary in honor of the founding in 1813, an annual event in the green time of the year, when young soloists and a chorus present a variety of masterpieces from Brahms, Beethoven, Haydn, Bach, or other classics as well as modern compositions. Actors present scenes from plays like *The Frogs* by Aristophanes or Gogol's *The Inspector General*. On the day I visited, the chorus sang Beethoven's "Kyrie" and "Agnus Dei" and selections from the oratorio *Samson* by Handel. I shall never forget the radiant faces of the choristers as they sang:

> Then round the starry throne
> Let their celestial concerts all unite.

The drama that day was *Der Gruftwächter* by Franz Kafka, when again the players transcended their blindness in their lines and in their movement about the stage.

The children in the elementary grades at the Institute have been singing for years too, but just now they are concentrating their energy and joy on the new Orff instruments.

In Williamsburg, Virginia, I found a poem that had been set to music in England in 1738, which expresses in old-fashioned words something of what these children are saying today through their music:

The Blind Boy

> O say, what is this thing called Light,
>   which I can ne'er Enjoy;
> What is the Blessing of the Light,
>   Oh! tell, tell your poor Blind Boy.

Music to "see" by.

With heavy Sighs I often hear
 You mourn my hopeless Woe,
But sure with Patience I may bear
 A Loss I ne'er can know.

Then let not what I cannot have
 My cheer of Mind destroy,
Whilst thus I Sing I am a King,
 Altho' a poor Blind Boy.[4]

  A choir is not a therapy group in the accepted meaning of the term. Its purpose involves providing an instrument

[4] Reprinted from George Bickham, Jr., *The Musical Entertainer* (London, 1738), verses 1, 4, 5, in the packet *Songs of Gentility*.

of worship for others as well as for the choir members, yet in practice it is a weekly renewal experience for the members whether they are children or adults. They come together by their own choice and the permission of the director, and both are acts of mutual trust and acceptance that give assurance of belonging. In singing together the members of a choir are united in a common purpose which is both upreaching and outgoing and so makes for wholeness. When a choirmaster gives himself as well as his talent, a spirit of fellowship develops that will deepen as time goes on, until it begins to dawn on the group that God is at work among them. In any church, large or small, when the choirs share this consciousness, the church as a whole is warmed by it, and responds. When word spread that our Youth Choir felt like second-rate citizens because they had no robes to wear, one of the couples in the church was moved to make a gift to cover the expense of a new robe for each member of the group. It was kept a secret until the Sunday morning they were to be presented. Without being told of the surprise, one of the boys in the Youth Choir was asked to lead his own group and the Adult Choir in singing a spiritual antiphonally: "I got a song, you got a song, all God's children got a song." When the time came, he led the children in those words for the first verse and gave the downbeat for the adults to sing the second verse: "I got a robe, you got a robe, all God's children got a robe." But they were silent. The boy was puzzled and tried again. Still nothing happened.

"We can't sing those words," explained the choirmaster, "because you folks *don't* have robes."

"But you *will* have," spoke up the minister, "right now."

Then it happened. To the complete astonishment of the children, they were called one by one from their places in the choir by the parents who came down the aisle bearing resplendent purple robes to be presented and put on then and there. Songs of rejoicing by the beaming children and the congregation rewarded the anonymous donors. It was one of those informal experiences that have the power to build trust in people and God and the Church.

An opportunity to build a relationship of trust may happen unexpectedly in one's own neighborhood. Lori was about five years old when we became friends. At first she came to my home as one of several children who dropped by now and then, when I had time to play games or get out the paint brushes. Later, when a homeless piano was moved into my kitchen, we had music. Then she began to come alone, too, and I learned that her need for friendship was very real. Her parents had been divorced and her mother worked. Stories, painting, and music were her delight, and especially two songs which she never tired of singing. One was the "Carol of Gratitude," a "thank you, Lord" song that children love because it covers things they can see, hear, do, and be. We dramatized special parts of it. For "bright colors in an autumn tree," we pointed at the maple through the window whether it was spring or fall, and for "all the friendly people when they smile at me," we turned to each other and grinned like Snoopy. For "jingle bells loud and clear," we kept a tiny Japanese temple bell at one end of the piano, and for "grateful for our life upon this little star," Lori cut one out of paper and taped it to a corner of the piano where she could point to it.

The other song required an active cast of two, which meant we had to sing without the piano.

> Hey! Hey! Anybody listening?
> Hey! Hey! Anybody there?
> Hey! Hey! Anybody listening?
> Anybody care? [5]

[5] © 1967, Richard K. Avery and Donald S. Marsh, *Hymns Hot and Carols Cool*. Used by permission.

The action as we developed it involved hiding and hunting and being found. The cue for the climax was "Anybody care?" at which the person who was hiding would jump out from behind the door or the chair or the shower curtain and shout, "*I* care!" Then the cast would hug each other to prove it.

There came a time when for a variety of reasons Lori was monster-ridden and filled with fear. She dropped in every day for a while and drew monsters. We also talked and sang the "I care" song. The monsters quickly grew less fearsome. There was even a good monster and a kind one, and a happy yellow snowman. We decided to make a "Book of Monsters by Lori" and I took down the things she wanted to say. This poem follows the drawing of a smiling cat:

> We laugh at the monster
> We laugh with the snowman
> because he knows how to laugh.
>
> Poor monster—
> he does not know how.
> But some day
> he will learn.
>
> Then he will laugh
> and we will laugh
> and everybody will laugh.

These thoughts have the ring of a dream and a prayer. They remind me of the first lines of Psalm 117 sung by the ancient Hebrews centuries ago and by us at Worldwide Communion recently:

> Praise the Lord, all nations!
> Praise the Lord, all people!

They also remind me of these words from an ancient Arapaho prayer chanted before there had been any contact between the Arapaho and whites:

> And we ask for all your peoples
> the growth of loving hearts
> and the happy life
> of peace and harmony.[6]

We were nearing the end of the "book" when Lori became very quiet for a time and then said slowly and thoughtfully: "Sometimes I *like* the monster. If I like him he will stay. If I don't like him he will go away. Scoot out!" The last two words were said with an emphatic gesture of dismissal, followed by silence once more. Then she summed it all up: "Sometimes we like them, sometimes we don't."

As though relieved by a confession, she reached for a sheet of pink paper and a pair of scissors and with a burst of energy cut out a huge heart and pasted it on the last page of the book.

"My heart and your heart," she said.

Then, taking another piece of paper, she began covering it with drawings of little hearts: "And I have a whole page of hearts to give to other people."

The crisis was over. Lori had moved quickly from fear to laughter to insight to love, and I think the monster may never be so big again, especially because the problems at home have been happily solved.

That experience suggests that songs for special stress should be available for children. Most homes have a well-stocked medicine cabinet ready for sniffles and sneezes, why not a music cabinet with songs for reassurance and encouragement? We have drugs for giving dreamless sleep,

[6] Tanslation by Benjamin Friday and William Shakespeare of the Wind River Reservation, Wyoming. Used by permission of St. Stephens Indian School, St. Stephens, Wyoming.

why not songs to keep their dreams alive? There are many to choose from and each family will want to choose their own, but here are a few suggestions: for nursery and kindergarten age, "God's Love Is Sure" (*Come Sing with Me*). For primaries in addition to the preschool group, "How Strong and Sure My Father's Care," "All God's Gifts Around Us," "God of Small Things" (*Sing for Joy*), and "I Like to Think of Jesus" (*Sing of Life and Faith*). Juniors, youth, and adults like "Morning Has Broken" in the same book, and any age can respond to "Hey! Hey! Anybody Listening?" "When I'm Feeling Lonely," and "Hosanna, Halleluia!" (*Hymns Hot and Carols Cool*). Everyone likes "He's Got the Whole World in His Hand," which is found in most contemporary songbooks, or "Stand by Me" and "Put Your Hand in the Hand," both in the *Genesis Songbook*.

For a healthy attitude toward nature, the song "Hi, Thunder" is a good one (*Sing Through the Day*). Both words and music are by children of the Macedonia Community of the Brothers. They address themselves playfully to the thunder and the sun, like well-known friends: "Hi, Thunder! Lo, Thunder! Hi, Sun! Lo, Sun! Come and play with us!" Just the song to sing with children who feel close to nature, and a healing song to sing with them if they are afraid of thunder.

In *Mr. Rogers' Songbook* (Random House) the song "I Like to Be Told" reminds us how important it is to prepare children in advance for new or difficult experiences. There are songs that parents and children can sing together that will help, such as "It's a Sad-happy Day When We Move Away" (*Come Sing with Me*). If a child knows that sometimes you can feel two different ways about the same thing, then if it happens to him, he will be more able to cope with the strangeness of it, and be on his way to developing attitudes of trust toward life, instead of fear.

When there is no crisis, family singing is still a good idea as a prevention of anxiety before it begins. It helps to create the kind of happiness that keeps monsters away. Recordings are good fun for singing games or rhythms or just quiet listening. Several families in our church in Port Jervis sing together regularly every day: old songs, new songs, folksongs, songs they learn at church. Some of these they act out, "I am the Church, You Are the Church" being one they especially like because there is a part for everyone.

In a bedtime ritual, the Butlers sing as they march around the diningroom table, Taffy the dog bringing up the rear. When it is time for prayers and quiet, they may sing a lullaby for Jesus which all but the youngest know by heart: "I'll rock you gentle, I'll rock you slow, rock you gentle to and fro. . . ." [7] The Gillettes sing along with their son's guitar which Todd learned to play after he discovered in the Orff group at the church what fun it is to play an

[7] © 1972, Richard K. Avery and Donald S. Marsh. "Baby Sitter," in *Songs for the Easter People.* Used by permission.

instrument. Music is a part of their lives, on a picnic, riding
in the car, at home, even in the bathtub. When the Schut-
tes play a record with a strong beat, all four may keep
time with their arms like a conductor. Favorites for this
are "Typewriter Song" and "Syncopated Clock" (L. Anderson) and "Take Time" (Avery and Marsh). Karen,
the youngest, will sometimes play records for over an hour
alone, singing, dancing, or swaying to the music. Her
brother Gary, began to write notes of music before he was
six.

The power of music is usually combined with other elements of healing, and most of us would hesitate to depend
on it alone, but for one man it was that or nothing, according to an account in *Better Music in the Church.*[8] E. P.
Scott was a missionary in India when he was captured by
a "murderous tribe" who pointed their spears toward his
heart. He fully expected to die until suddenly he remembered his violin and managed to get it into playing position.
Closing his eyes he played "All Hail the Power of Jesus'
Name" and sang the words softly. At the last verse, "Let
every kindred, every tribe," he opened his eyes to discover
that the tribe's attitude had completely changed. In gratitude he remained there and served these people for more
than two years.

In ways beyond our comprehension music is a universal
language, not in theory but in fact. Research indicates that
the childhood chants we hear on our playgrounds and in
our own backyards are the same as those of children
around the world. The pentatonic scale is basic in many
folktunes and singing games. When I visited a Kodály
workshop at Chautauqua, New York, I realized that the
structure of music represents a truth as fundamental as the
Torah. If a chord is two steps apart at the top of the piano,

[8] O. W. Moerner, *Better Music in the Church.* © 1939 by the Cokesbury Press, Nashville, Tenn.

it will be the same at the bottom. You can depend on it. Life is meant to be sane! Yet happily there is change in the vibration and there are many kinds of intervals and rhythms for variety and beauty. Life is meant to be creative! Like Torah, music has both authority and movement.

When I saw Roberta Flack on television leading the audience at one of the Boston Pops concerts, I saw the change that took place on the faces of thousands of people as they sang "I Believe in Music, I Believe in Love." At first some of them hesitated to give themselves to the joy of that spirit and kept right on looking worried, fearful, aloof. But she kept at them with the words and her spirit, "Sing it with me, children," until the music was nearly a unanimous experience.

I like to think that when children or adults sing in a choir or in a congregation on Sunday morning, it is a healing affirmation of a covenant between God and all who will accept it, that life is worth living and life is worth giving.

7

The Heritage Is Now

W E A R E alive only in the present tense, not yesterday or tomorrow but now. It is always so. It was "now" to Abraham when he sickened of the mess of gods and goddesses in his hometown and broke with its confusion, convinced that God is One. In an act of complete trust he moved his family and servants and animals and household goods to a far country and began again. It was "now" when Moses beheld the suffering of his people embodied so sharply in a single incident that he killed a man in reflex anger, and it was "now" when he gained perspective as a fugitive and perceived the Holy in the "burning bush," answering reluctantly the call not to kill the enemy but to lead his own people.

The days of Jeremiah, Jesus, Paul, and St. Augustine were all "now" to them, and when we understand them, they become a part of our own life even in the last quarter of the twentieth century, not a distant fact separated by time and language and custom. The scene does change, but the basic human drama is somehow strangely familiar. Not so long ago I too woke up to the fact that the New

Testament is *now*. For that matter so is the Old Testament.
I went to the piano and drew my hand over the keys from
bottom to top in the consciousness that I was making a
leap of two thousand years. Twice that, if you go back to
Abraham, as I think we must if our heritage is to be complete. When God is One, so are His people, and time has
little to do with our essential nature.

We know from their behavior in the wilderness that
the people of Israel, like all humanity, sometimes followed
God, sometimes forgot Him. Yet in spite of their weak-
ness and sin, or perhaps because of it, He entrusted them
with a gift of priceless value to them and to all the world:
the Torah, or Law. It guided them through their struggles
for some twelve hundred years before the birth of Christ
and has continued to guide them for nearly two thousand
years since. Without it there might have been no national
glory under David and Solomon. Without it Amos would
have had no basis for his moral judgment, as sorely needed
then as by us today.

Strangely enough, there are few if any songs in Christian hymnals to celebrate this costly gift. Is it because we
think of the Law as being fulfilled in Jesus Christ and so
pass over it as nothing to sing about? If so, I think this is
a mistake. Jesus did say he came to fulfill the Law, but he
could not have done that if there had been no Law to
fulfill.

In his book *Torah and Canon*, James Sanders suggests
that it was the memory of Torah that kept Israel's identity
alive even in exile and dispersion, a power it possesses because it is a story remembered and retold again and again,
the story of the acts of God in favor of His people. Israel
believed God had saved them in the past and believed He
would continue to do so. The Torah is the "gospel" of the
Old Testament, writes Dr. Sanders, and has the flexibility
if we will update our dialogue with it, to help each suc-

ceeding generation answer for itself the two crucial questions: "Who am I?" and "What am I to do?"

With this in mind, it is exciting to read between the lines in the second chapter of Ezra, which describes the return of fifty thousand refugees from their exile in Babylon. Among them were the Levites and the trained singers, about two hundred leaders in music. It is safe to say they led the people in song as they made their long trek back to Jerusalem. Can we not say they survived remembering, believing, and *singing*? And obviously, going somewhere.

It is fascinating to realize that their music was not only a remembering. It was also a borrowing. Possibly something from the Assyrians whose music was flourishing at the time, but certainly from the Egyptians among whom the Hebrews had lived earlier for four hundred years. Scholars surmise the music along the Nile was both beautiful and strong because of the instruments the Egyptians carved on their monuments: the harp, the trumpet, cymbals and the like, the same instruments that the Hebrews used in the Temple later in Jerusalem. They may have borrowed from the music itself as well, for the Egyptians had developed elaborate worship rituals in their own temples, including trained choruses accompanied by instruments. In fact, the Pharaohs appointed a man to serve as superintendant of singing.

Cultures do meet in spite of differences and antagonisms, and sometimes unpredictably, like a sudden chuckle in the cosmos. Even tunes or musical patterns for pagan worship in Greece were adapted for Catholic worship. "Hymn to the Sun" became the basis for an "Alleluia," and the historians tell us there are signs of "Hymn to Nemesis" in one of the Kyries. Though most of the ancient tunes cannot be identified now, many of the instruments they were played on are still with us in museums or even in active use. Nubians on the upper Nile today are said to play the lyre in the same way that the Greeks did a thousand years ago. We owe much to the Greeks musically.

In a previous chapter we referred to the Greeks' strong belief in the power of music to influence human life for good. They were also the first people in Europe to study music and try to work out a system of notation using symbols over the notes to indicate rhythm. This laid the foundation for music as we understand it today. If the oriental musicians had done that, later generations would have been enriched.

As it was, the music of the Hebrew faith must have had considerable influence on the stream of Christian song. In the early days before the persecutions, those of the new faith continued to worship publicly in the Temple and the local synagogues. Changes do not happen all at once. But as the status quo changed and antagonisms developed between Christians and Romans and Jews, Christians began to realize the need to develop their own worship ways which would express directly their relationship to Jesus Christ. By the sixth century the Catholic Church was secure enough to borrow from the biblical cantillation of the Hebrews when they developed the Gregorian Chant. Edward Dickinson thinks the early Christians may have had a few folksongs of their own as well as hymns written in Latin, though we cannot be sure because they had to be sung secretly and were probably never written down. There is a tradition that the earliest Christian hymn is "Lux Beator" (O Blessed Light). We do not even know the names of those who worshiped in the catacombs with the exception of one patrician woman, Cecelia, who was killed by Roman soldiers and later was made the patron saint of music.

In Greece, the Christians had a quite different experience. Emotion ran high in their assemblies and they are said to have expressed their feelings in wordless shouts and exclamations of joy which approached the sound of music, as though a muffling of praise in one city released it in another like a safety valve. Along with other forms of praise, this ecstatic "gift of tongues" is said to have entered the stream of devotional music somehow, affecting change and being itself changed in the process. It has been suggested, for example, that the Catholic "Jubilation" music may owe something to the gift of tongues.

Whether or not this is so, we do know from the history of music in general and church music in particular that there is a continuing ebb and flow of influence which is sometimes called the Tidal Law. It is necessary to know this if we are to comprehend the music of our own time.

We wonder if it ever crossed the minds of those meeting in the catacombs by torchlight that they were inaugurating the first Christian church music, the beginning of a custom that would go through many changes and be hotly debated for generations to come, but would continue to be a force for understanding and renewal to Christians around the world. Or did the Christians who practiced antiphonal music from Mesopotamia to Libya on the African coast remember that they were indebted to the Hebrew custom of using two choirs responsively in the Temple? All ancient Christian music was vocal and women sang in the choirs at first, but were excluded in the sixth century except in the convents. Had they been misbehaving? Or did they not dare to protest that women living six hundred years after Jesus ought to be allowed the same privilege that Miriam and the other Hebrew women enjoyed some thirteen hundred years before his birth? Or were the times so unsettled that the only hope of survival lay in tightened authority and responsibility? History can make us humble as well as anxious. It is true the times were indeed unsettled.

No sooner had Constantine put a stop to the persecution than he built a city on the site of old Byzantium and named it after himself. This brought the tides of Rome and the East together in a new way less than a hundred years before the fall of Rome. When that happened, early in the fifth century, the Barbarians from the north swarmed in and everyone who had lived under the umbrella of Roman law and order was confronted with the beginning of change. This was the beginning of the Dark Ages in Western Europe. Dedicated Christians responded with missionary zeal. In the sixth century, Columba set out from Ireland to convert the savage Scots, and St. Augustine went west to convert the heathen in south Britain. He is said to have been so deeply moved by the new church music prepared earlier by Ambrose and now by Pope Gregory the Great, that he wept for joy and then felt guilty for fear he was enjoying the tune at the expense of the message. It was Ambrose who had defined a hymn simply as "a song in praise of the Lord."

The new music represented a break with pagan art, for it turned from the old Greek emphasis on rhythm to letting melody dominate, thus making church style distinct from the secular. The ideal was to express a universal mood of prayer rather than individualized emotion.

Just how much of a treasure this new music was felt to be is indicated by the fact that the hymns and chants were copied on vellum in a large leather volume and fastened to the altar of St. Peter's Church in Rome with a gold chain where people came from long distances to see them. The words were from the Psalms and took so much skill to sing that the congregation was not equal to it and special choirs had to be trained in singing schools. Apparently the withdrawal of singing from the congregation was not, in the beginning at least, an arbitrary act of authority but a practical measure which had grown out of the sense of need for music worthy of the Church.

A statement made to church singers at the Council of Carthage in the fourth century throws light on the situation: "See that what thou singest with thy lips thou believest in thy heart; and what thou believest in thy heart thou dost exemplify in thy life." The statement went on to say that the Church had need to cherish the genius of her children and to use her imagination and skill to add "beauty, dignity and fitness to her ordinances of worship." Plainsong or Gregorian Chant seemed to satisfy these requirements for many generations.

Toward the end of the eighth century, a few years before he was crowned first emperor of the Holy Roman Empire, Charlemagne ordered a collection of songs made for each locality so that people could enjoy together their own local songs about spinning, drinking, weddings, brave deeds, and the like. There were Scandinavian, Welsh, Irish, French, Spanish, and German songs before the people were "nationals" in the later sense. Charlemagne was ahead of his time in realizing the importance of music to a community. The Church used some of these tunes, but when people began to stamp their feet and express the urge to dance, church authorities felt the tunes were too lively to be appropriate.

Many homeless people often took to the road, some earning their living by acrobatic stunts and singing. These professional "minstrels" brought news as they went from town to town. Their audiences were travelers in the tavern courtyards, noblemen and their servants at the castles, or pilgrims on their way to some shrine. Most of these wanderers were poor and got a bad reputation for stealing. Both the state and the Church called them "lawless fellows" and required them to identify themselves by special outfits of bright-colored stripes or checks. For a time they were made to wear their hair long, and in Basle were forbidden to wear trousers. If hired by a lord, they wore bells on their caps and carried scepters. Although minstrels were considered socially inferior, Crusaders often took them along to the Holy Land to lessen their own boredom.

Some of these knights brought home instruments new to the West, like the lute, mandolin, guitar, and fiddle. Some say the oboe we enjoy in the symphony orchestra found its way to the West at that time. A few Crusaders who were gifted poets were inspired to compose new songs of love with new melodies and rhythms. Some of these men became troubadours when they returned home, aristocrats among the performers.

Apparently they wrote no songs of penitence for the thousands that were killed, fifty thousand in one battle alone, or for the many children who died along the way. Not even St. Bernard of Clairvaux raised his voice in protest, says Phyllis McGinley in *Saint Watching*, probably because the capture of Jerusalem by Islam looked like the end of Christian civilization unless the city could be won back.

The jugglers, in contrast, were of the people, some of them clerical dropouts from the Church. The irony was that knights who were near the top of the social ladder were often illiterate, like most people before the printing press, and to get their own songs written down, accepted the help of these same jugglers, many of whom could both read and write.

In medieval abbeys and monasteries, the purity of the chants was maintained in the singing of the liturgy, the daily prayers or "offices" and in Grace at table. "At the end of the meal," reads one story about these times, "the monks rose and sang grace before they marched out through the long arched walks of the cloister. Louis enjoyed moving in a quiet rhythm with the other black-robed monks along the arched walks. He enjoyed the rise and fall of their voices as they chanted." [1] In a Benedictine monastery in the Mosel region of West Germany, one

[1] Irma Simonton Black, *Castle, Abbey and Town.* © 1963 by Holiday House, Inc. Used by permission.

can still hear the beauty of such a chant at Vespers. On the day I was there, the summer sun was shining as the men moved in procession from their dormitory to the chapel, singing. The effect was otherworldly until another Brother came in sight on a bicycle coasting down the road with a basket of vegetables, very much of the earth here and now. In New York, the boys at the Choir School of St. John the Divine sing Grace at table, and it is the most beautiful singing Grace I have ever heard.

Jewish communities living in many different areas in the Middle Ages maintained their music. In all except Poland, strict rules were laid down to keep the songs and chants authentic. In Poland, for some reason, more freedom was permitted and variations began to appear. Objections were raised that song leaders were using the opportunity to promote themselves rather than their faith.

So it went, the ebb and flow of old and new forms in music, the ebb and flow of events in history for good or ill.

The beautiful cathedral at Salisbury had scarcely been completed when the horrors of the fourteenth century descended. The Black Death spread over Europe killing a third of the population in two and a half years, wiping out whole towns in a few days. The dead piled up unburied and social conditions were unspeakable. Chivalry was in decay, fashion was absurd, there was cynicism and despair. Yet church bells went on ringing, and choirs sang in Salisbury. The Mastersingers were formed in Germany, simple harmony was finding its way into music as "rounds," called "canons" in the Church. These were gaining popularity in England and would grow up to be "fugues" centuries later with Bach to nourish them.

Chaucer was writing the outstanding poetry of the age, and at the turn of the century a man would be born on the Continent who would bring new life to the world by the invention of the printing press. No longer would monks have to spend their lives copying the Scriptures by hand, and think what it would mean in making music available! The Renaissance was already here, America was soon to be discovered, and the Reformation was just around the corner in the sixteenth century.

Barbara Tuchman has said that the reporting of an event multiplies by ten the impression that it represents a permanent situation in society, and mentions that neither Chaucer nor the author of *Piers Plowman* referred to the Plague at all.[2] They had other things they wanted to say. Someone had to tell the horror "like it was," but we can be grateful that Chaucer raised his voice alongside and let us know how well he understood the pilgrims on their way to Canterbury and how much he loved them anyway.

Perhaps the fourteenth century helped prepare the way for the new life in church music made possible by Martin Luther. He saw congregational singing as a symbol of the believer's direct access to God. What an event it must have been to sing out together in those early days of the Reformation! God was nearer than people had dreamed. He was on their side without any barrier, not even a priest. The typical Lutheran hymn was a "chorale," a lyric sometimes set to a tune from a secular melody easy for people to sing together. Like John Wesley and General Booth, Luther crossed the "forbidden frontier" between sacred and secular music. "Let it be music," he remarked, "we will make it as sacred as need be."

Stories grew up about the amount of original writing and composing of hymns Luther did. Actually he was more of an adapter of tunes and words than an originator. The first hymnbook of Evangelical Germany contained four hymns by Luther, another the same year contained

[2] "History as Mirror," *The Atlantic Monthly*, September 1973.

fourteen, and by 1543, thirty-six of his hymns had been published in all, although only five of these were original. Even "Ein Feste Burg," which was one of these, borrowed from Psalm 46 and had a little flavor of Gregorian chant. Luther's real contribution to church music was his witness to the power of faith and freedom in the authority of God and the love of Jesus Christ, and his grasp of the necessity to give the people a way to express this in song.

As soon as Luther founded the new church in Wittenberg, people celebrated their release in outbursts of singing. They had inherited the temperament for music, and Luther, the son of a peasant, understood their vigorous language. He also knew the music they were already familiar with and borrowed from both the Latin songs of the Catholic Church and the secular tunes. He redesigned the liturgy to stress active participation of the people rather than submission to formality. He saw the needs of the time and tried to express what people had been longing for in words they could understand, in songs and in sermons. People caught the message all across the land, and it resounded with sounds of faith and hope that went to the heart. One Catholic is said to have remarked that the people were singing themselves into the Lutheran faith. Heine called "Ein Feste Burg" the "Marseillaise of the Reformation." He said, "Patriotic and moral fire burns in this mighty song."

Then came the eighteenth century in England when congregational singing played an important role in the rise of Methodism. People had become aware of the shocking conditions in moral and social life. Hogarth was drawing his memorable cartoons, one of which showed a man hanging himself in a garret, while a woman on the street below poured gin down the throat of an infant in her arms. The Wesleys came forward, John preaching and Charles writing songs, and both promoting strict rules of

personal discipline. History credits the Methodist movement wth sobering England up in time to prevent national
disaster. People took to drinking tea instead of gin,
and Charles kept on writing songs—seven thousand of
them—putting Gospel words to street ballad tunes that
caught on in the mines, on the farms, and on the city
streets.

Today we are being stirred to new ways in both music
and worship. The heritage is "now" and we see parallels in
our own day with the past. History affects music and music
influences history in the world at large, in the Church, and
in the personal lives of individuals. This is why it is sad
that some public schools in America offer children so little
in the way of music. The real reason for occasional neglect
may be not so much the lack of money as the lack of
understanding. If those responsible for the education of
children really knew how intimately music is related to
our lives as human beings, they would recognize it as a
creative force indispensable to our well-being rather than a
luxury item that is the first to go when a curriculum is cut.
Primitive people have sensed this in a more practical way
than many of us who call ourselves civilized. At one time
American Indian mothers carried their small children on
their hips when they danced, not so much as a baby-
sitting device as to instill in them an awareness of rhythm.
A similar custom is practiced today by many women in
Africa. Our choir rehearsals in Port Jervis often include
infants by necessity, but even so, they are a future heritage.

Here and there, happily, are growing signs of concern
that music be made more available to children. Public
school teachers are showing keen interest in attending
music conferences and workshops over the weekend or
at summer sessions. Some teachers study at the Musical
Training Institute in Wellesley, Massachusetts, where the
Kodály concept of music is presented. Hearing the Suzuki

children from Japan play their violins may have increased an interest in providing instrument instruction in the elementary public schools, although the average American child does not take readily to the kind of discipline the Suzuki method requires. For developmental reasons, our preschools prefer to start music with rhythmics and singing. Children and parents who attend· the Yamaha classes sponsored by a commercial firm are enthusiastic about both the instruction and the spirit in the groups. A favorite song is one that expresses the welcome thought that there's music in both me and you! So we can be grateful to those who come to us as missionaries of music, so to speak.

It was especially encouraging to read in the Port Jervis *Union Gazette* (Feb. 26, 1974) that one of the schools in the Tri-States area is developing a far-sighted program of

ED ECKSTEIN

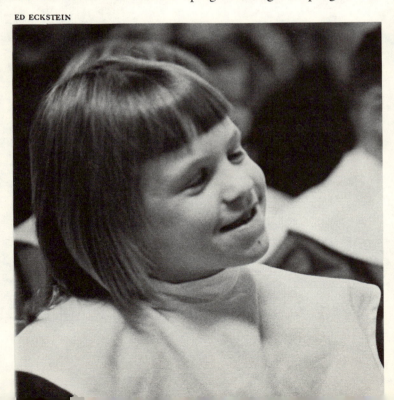

music as a regular part of the curriculum. It will progress from instruction suitable at the kindergarten and early primary levels to sight-singing, two-part harmony and so on, up through the eighth grade where music history will be presented. Experiments in relating music to the other arts are carried on and students are encouraged to develop their creative interests in singing, drama, rock opera, or dance.

It is worthy of note that some churches now provide music education in addition to their choir programs. Among these are the University Heights Presbyterian Church in the Bronx, New York City, where children of a multi-ethnic neighborhood may learn to read music and play an instrument; and the Central Christian Church of Danville, Illinois, whose novel team ministry makes music instruction possible for both youth and adults.

The twentieth century has been called the "choral century" to distinguish it from the nineteenth-century emphasis on the orchestra. Glee Clubs may have disappeared from many colleges, but not from the secondary schools, although they may not be called by that name. Here and there independent groups are flourishing, like the Newark Boys' Chorus, and outstanding example of what group singing can do for those involved in it. The boys perform their art with a high degree of excellence and have a relationship with each other in which differences of race are neither a barrier nor a source of competition. One gets the impression their love of music and their joy in performing it together make those other matters a bore as far as they are concerned.

From Boggs Academy in Georgia, a co-ed choir of thirty-six talented black students of highschool age makes an annual tour that often takes them into seven states to sing a wide variety of music that includes the classics, folk-songs, and spirituals. Their rehearsal schedule is demanding but they accept it rather than miss a trip, and their account-ability shows up in purity of tone and excellent diction.

A choir in El Paso, Texas, goes traveling too. Although the choir program in the First Presbyterian Church begins with the first grade, it is the Youth Choir and the Adult Choir that join for the tours. They have given five concerts at Our Lady of Guadaloupe Cathedral in Juarez, Mexico, and during the six years since they were organized by Bruce Nehring, the organist-director, have sung in Wisconsin, Oregon, New England, Colorado, and Canada, paying for most of their own travel expenses. A growing number of Mexican-American youth are involved in the regular weekly program, which may include the finest music in choral literature as well as simple ballads and folksongs.

Most readers will have heard of the Berkshire Boys' Choir that sang in Bernstein's "Mass" at the opening of the John F. Kennedy Center for the Performing Arts in Washington, and the Texas Girls' Choir of Fort Worth that has sung in many countries including the Holy Land. We accept for granted the excellence of the boys' choirs at St. John the Divine in New York or Trinity Church in Princeton. but may not yet have heard of the Mennonite Children's choir in Winnipeg, Canada, that undertook to sponsor one hundred needy children in celebration of the tenth anniversary of their founding. We may hear of the outstanding work being done by the Choral Society in Charlotte, North Carolina, or the dedication of the adult singers in a Bach Chorus, such as the one that performs annually in Bethlehem, Pennsylvania; yet the growing edge in choral music is in the church at the grass roots, where choirs for all ages are growing in size and expanding in number.

If anyone has not yet become aware of this, a reading of the Choristers Guild Letters published each month will be an adventure in discovery. For choir directors, it is also a clearinghouse of material both practical and creative, in articles, book reviews, exchange of ideas, presentation of new music, reports on workshops and seminars, but best of all it is a sharing of a spirit of hope and joy. A file of back numbers is a veritable reference library for a choir. I have just come across the issue for October 1970, in which Helen Kemp, who was then director of workshops and festivals for the Guild, shared some of her discoveries in working with children's choirs: how to feel out each personality unobtrusively to discover the practical needs in music learning as well as in personal traits of response—shy? overly eager?—how boys like to go into a "huddle" to talk things over, how you can keep a long-held note in tune by slowly pointing a finger up while singing. She advised the children to avoid "breathing scared," which is really "shallow chest panting," and suggested that imitating a fire siren helps warm up the voice, and the free swing of a jump-rope is an aid in learning steady rhythm.

Before going to Dallas to work with the Choristers Guild, Dr. and Mrs. Kemp were co-ministers of music for nineteen years in a church with an outstanding program of graded choirs. Now they are on the faculty of the Westminster Choir College in Princeton. Because of their

professional teamwork, they have also had noteworthy
experiences with their own five children as they were
growing up, beginning with blessings at table and bedtime
prayers, singing simple tunes from Beethoven, Bach, and
Mozart. They also sang together in the car on vacation
trips—rounds, canons, folktunes. Then came family concerts at the church. Finally, in 1962–63, the entire family
journeyed to Holland to study trends in music in western
Europe. They lived near The Hague, and from time to
time delighted large audiences with their family concerts.
Now several of their children are involved in music professionally, and the grandchildren are experiencing the
daily joy of music as a way of life. So Good News moves
from one generation to another. Alleluia!

When the American Guild of Organists held its national
convention in 1972 at Southern Methodist University in
Dallas, Texas, the "happy opening event" was a celebration in Perkins Chapel called "Sounds of Singing Children."
It was sponsored by the Choristers Guild and the children
were girls and boys selected from the junior choirs of the
Dallas churches. Sounds from the past and present were
imaginatively joined in the program as a reprint of it
below will indicate.

SOUNDS OF SINGING CHILDREN
Helen Kemp, conductor
Phil Baker, accompanist

Introit and Procession . . . . Hal Hopson
Unison voices, brass quartet, organ

SOUNDS FROM THE PAST
Come and Thank Him . . . . Johann Sebastian Bach
From the Christmas Oratorio
In Thee, O Lord, Is Fullness of
Joy . . . . Francois Couperin

What Is the Joyful News? ....Carl Gerhardt
*A little Christmas cantata for unison
voices, recorders, and continuo*

SOUNDS TO CELEBRATE TODAY
Four anthems composed for this event by
John Burke—Austin Lovelace
Jane Marshall—Dale Wood

SOUNDS FOR THE POPULAR NOW
100% Chance of Rain
(inspired by Noah) ....Walter Horsley
*A premiere performance of a jazz cantata
for children, piano, flutes, percussion,
and string bass*

SOUNDS FOR CREATIVE LISTENING
A Joyous Psalm ....Eugene Butler
Remember Your Creator ....Samuel Adler
Little Grey Donkey .. .. Natalie Sleeth
Christmas Is the Harvest Time of
Love ....Wilma Jensen

Procession Into the World—Alleluia! ..John Kemp
Choir, congregation, brass, and organ

Still another way to bring the past and the present
together is in a "Service of Hymns" which involves the
congregation at regular Sunday morning worship. How
it can be made more significant than the "old-fashioned
hymn sing" was described in the feature articles of the
Guild newsletter, "In the Worship Workshop with Avery
and Marsh," for June 1973. A narrator, usually the minister,
tells the origin of each hymn and something of the life of
the writer before the congregation sings it. The hymns are
grouped according to a theme, or the life of Jesus, or God
and Creation, or experiences of human faith. Sometimes a

soloist will sing one of the stanzas or an instrument will be introduced for variety. The organ prelude is usually related to the hymn tunes, and sometimes the stanzas are read responsively or in unison. In Port Jervis, we gather once or twice a year with a neighboring church for this kind of service and it is always a time of fellowship and renewal. A sample of one of the services is printed on page 199.

For these occasions there are songs related to the core of teaching in the New Testament, but not many for the old Testament except for hymns based on psalms. There are few that relate to the prophets or the major episodes of the Torah that brought life to Israel in a crisis. In a search through fourteen books of Christian hymns and songs I found only a handful: "The God of Abraham Praise," "For Man's Unceasing Quest for God," "Passed thru the Waters," "Go Down, Moses," "By the Babylonian Rivers," and "O God of the Eternal Now." Two verses of this last one are quoted to indicate how a modern hymn can relate to the ancient Torah:

> May we with courage take the risk
> to leave the past behind,
> to be a people on the move,
> throw caution to the wind.

> Give us the heart of Abraham,
> for changes make us bold;
> and bless us only so that we
> in turn may bless the world.[3]

All but the first two songs above use symbols of the Old Testament to present teachings of the New, and this is valid as a part of trying to "up-date" the dialogue for ourselves, but to get the Jews' own feeling for the Torah, the best

[3] "O God of the Eternal Now," by Frederik Herman Kaan, *The Hymn Book*. Copyright 1971 by the Anglican Church and the United Church of Canada. Used by permission.

way I know is to attend worship at a synagogue service. The Reader who leads the preparation for opening the Ark where the Torah is kept chants melodies and prayers that have come down to the cantors for generations. As the Ark is opened, the congregation rises, and there is no mistaking the depth of their feeling for the gift of Torah. The Shema is then repeated by everyone in unison: "Hear, O Israel, the Lord our God is one Lord" (Deuteronomy 6:4).

Think what these words mean for Christians as well as Jews: freedom from the confusion of multiple gods and goddesses! Abraham won that battle about four thousand years ago, and every Christian and every Jew is heir to that victory if he wishes to be. The song "The God of Abraham Praise," mentioned above, refers to this oneness of God:

> Who was, and is, and is to be,
> And still the same!
> The one eternal God,
> Ere aught that now appears;
> The First, the Last: beyond all thought
> His timeless years! [4]

It is a translation from a Jewish Doxology, or hymn of praise, called a "Yigdal," a form still heard in daily services in many synagogues in America. This tune appears in Christian hymnbooks, some with the ancient words intact, others in a modified version. Surely Christians can recognize that although for us the meaning of the hymn may expand the ancient words, they are not thereby canceled out. Our roots go back to them as Jesus' did, and our children can learn much from singing them and lose much by not doing so.

[4] "The God of Abraham Praise," words by Daniel ben Judah about A. D. 1400. In the *Pilgrim Hymnal* © 1958, The Pilgrim Press.

Prayers and responses made at Festivals before the open Ark are beautiful and moving. Among the prayers used at Passover, the two here quoted from would be meaningful in Christian worship because the release from Egypt is part of Christian history too, and part of Christian joy.

> We thank thee, O our Father, for the joy and gladness of this Festival. . . . Thou didst bring us forth from slavery to freedom, from darkness to light, from human bondage to Thy divine service. . . .[5]

The second prayer goes beyond rejoicing for their own release to a vision of worldwide liberty which sounds much like the Christian hope for the Kingdom of heaven on earth:

> O God and Redeemer, may the portion of Torah we read on this Festival of Freedom bring hope unto all who are oppressed and renew their faith in Thy saving power. Thou who desirest that all men be free, didst enjoin upon us to proclaim liberty to all the inhabitants of the earth. May that day soon come, O Lord, when all Thy children shall be liberated from bondage, and free men everywhere unite in rendering homage unto Thee. Amen.[6]

These prayers help us to see that the law of the Old Testament, far from being outside the realm of love, is essential to its foundation. To help write this concept on the heart, Christian adults as well as children could learn to sing the second verse of "The God of Abraham Praise":

[5] From *The Sabbath and Festival Prayer Book.* © 1946, The Rabbinical Assembly and the United Synagogue of America. Used by permission of the publisher.
[6] Ibid.

His spirit floweth free,
High surging where it will;
In prophet's word he spoke of old
He speaketh still.

Established is his law,
And changeless it shall stand,
Deep writ upon the human heart,
On sea, or land.

When they understand that "Law" is more than the Ten
Commandments, that it includes all the stories that show
God's continuing concern for His people, it could be a
song of reconciliation. Children would enjoy singing it
with a drum or tambourine, or a clapping rhythm. If a
visit to the local synagogue could be arranged, it would
crown the meaning of the song, especially if we make the
two prayers quoted above our own.

The sculptor Jacob Lipschitz believed in the importance
of interfaith understanding while still maintaining one's
own tradition. His statue, "The Descent of the Spirit,"
now in the cloister court of the restored abbey on the
Island of Iona, bears this inscription:

I, Jacob Lipschitz, a Jew faithful to the faith of my
fathers, have made this Virgin for a good understanding
among all the people of the earth. That the Spirit may
reign.

In the epilogue of James Sanders' *Torah and Canon*
there is this further statement of hope: "For Judaism,
Torah became the living Talmud; for Christianity, Torah
became the living Christ. But Torah can finally never be
lost or absorbed in the one or the other." This should re-
assure both Jews and Christians that it is safe to talk with
each other.

We are in another high moment of history. The heritage
is now. What shall we give the future? If we know our
kinship with the past and yet are not possessed by it, so
that we can see how far we are from where we have to
go, we may learn the kind of music that will help to make
a future possible.

> Living Lord, renew the charge
> at your rising given:
> that the church in love should bring
> to this life your heaven.
> Give us insight, show us how
> life is here, the task is now.[7]

[7] From "Jesus, Shepherd of Our Souls," by Erik Routley and
Frederik H. Kaan. in *The Hymn Book*, © 1971 by the Anglican
Church and the United Church of Canada. Used by permission.

8

Music In a Changing World

M U S I C helps people to weather change. During the last twenty years or so the Church has had experiences that brought doubt and anguish, and during the last ten, serious conflict and confusion. Some have faced violence and rioting in the streets, some more subtle confrontations within their own household. National church assemblies have made hard decisions causing pain and separation, but the churches I know best have all survived. The cautious and the daring have found a common meeting ground through their sense of history and their commitment, although with varying interpretations, to Jesus Christ as Lord. All have been upheld by the vitality of music. If God is love, then I think the Holy Spirit is music.

When change came some years ago to the First Presbyterian Church in Greenwich, Connecticut, through the death of a beloved elderly pastor, the handful of members —some sixty or so—decided they wanted to expand and build for a new day. The experts who came and surveyed their "growth potential" shook their heads and said in effect: "Nothing doing. Better sit tight." But the people were not content with that and got busy in their own way. Five years later they had a remodeled church and a new educational building, and ten years later nearly a thousand members. Now there are almost fifteen hundred, thanks to the faith and hard work of the dedicated members and the distinguished ministers whom they have called to serve.

Many elements must have entered into the new growth: golf to get acquainted, sermons to challenge thinking, and the building of more modest housing as the back-country estates began to divide. An active volunteer choir was quite certainly significant. During the unsettled days when the building was being remodeled, the choir must have given the congregation a feeling of stability on Sunday mornings. When old doors were being closed off and new ones opened up, the choir was there and singing. When paint was being scraped off the old beams and people were pleased to see the true beauty of the wood revealed, the choir was there to lead the songs of praise.

One of the regular singers in the group was Bud Collyer, the late television star, who also taught the high school class before church. "Go out with your date on Saturday night," he would say, "but be here on Sunday morning." And they were, fifty or sixty of them, some of them becoming interested in the choir.

As new members joined the church, the choir celebrated their coming as well as the sacraments and the festivals of the church year, the weddings and the funerals. As the church grew, the choir grew, and as the choir grew so did the church. In fact it was life including death that was being celebrated—the comings and the goings, the weeping and rejoicing, commitments, honors, memorials—and all were in some way shared and supported by the choir.

When Bud Collyer died, the choir sang at the service for him in the church, and one of his daughters who was a member of it sang as usual, a witness to her own faith and her father's. He had dedicated a book of poems to his three children "who taught me so much that I needed to know." No wonder one of his children wanted to sing in the choir to his memory. Communication from one generation to another had apparently been a two-way affair in their family. One of the poems in the second section refers to that "sun-filled day"

> When generation talks to generation,
> Each hearing what the other has to say.[1]

This can happen in the wider church family too, and did in Greenwich recently when the Junior Choir, now grown to fifty, sang a psalm to music improvised by the organist: "Clap your hands for joy." Other children danced in the aisles, clapping the rhythm with such infectious joy that the parents forgot formality and clapped along with them. A little child can lead us all.

There have been other innovations, such as a choir concert with the help of Haydn and a chamber orchestra, and a presentation of Leonard Bernstein's "Chichester Psalms." Currently, the congregation is gathering strength for another step which the present minister, the Reverend George Pera, hopes will result in a new center for early childhood and youth groups. Space at the church has been outgrown again. Their own interest in the new quarters has been dramatized by the Primary children with a procession to the "Promised Land," the site of the hoped-for building, bearing "grapes" for food in the form of raisins. Although on a different level of need, this reminds one of the musical *Raisin* and the hit song, which is a prayer by the mother for a home in a better neighborhood.

The winds of change have always blown in Washington,

---

[1] Bud Collyer, *With the Whole Heart.* Copyright © 1966, by Fleming H. Revell Company. Use by permission.

D.C., and the New York Avenue Presbyterian Church, in the heart of the District, has lived through many crises, including the Civil War. I doubt if the members have ever taken any of them casually, for they enjoy strong opinions, and controversy flourishes. In the church school on Sunday morning there are now seven adult classes, each dealing with a different facet of the Gospel. During a recent six-week series two groups studied Paul and his message and the others explored the following concerns: "What it means to be a church member," "The theology of social action," "Jews and Christians," "Liberation theology," "Christian theology and living experience: beliefs for all seasons." Diversity in accord, a kind of music of the mind.

If the door of the Nursery Class should open during these discussions, the sound of children's voices might be heard singing a favorite song:

> Love one another,
> Love one another,
> Love one another,
> Jesus said.[2]

Fortunately, words do get translated into many kinds of service. Volunteers teach, sing in the choir, serve as neighborhood visitors, cooperate with people of other faiths to help provide food for hungry people, join a task force to study some issue of the day and report back, or tutor children of the inner city, which is perhaps the most unusual of the projects. It has been in operation for twelve years, one night each week. Some fifty or sixty children and youth attend, and since the tutoring is on a one-to-one basis, there are about one hundred people busily at work in the fifth-floor study hall every Thursday night.

This activity is coordinated with the public schools and

[2] "Love One Another" by Edith Sloane. In *Sing for Joy* © 1961, The Seabury Press. Used by permission.

the church Community Club, whose members are required to participate in the study program unless their school records show they do not need it. The club is open three days a week from four o'clock until nine, and the members enjoy the challenge of running the club themselves, with an adult available for counsel. How well interest has been sustained is shown when some of the graduates return to serve as tutors themselves.

Arts and crafts have been introduced, and it is hoped that music will be added. Tutors and students are encouraged to get acquainted as friends, and informal activities outside the church building range from movies and picnics to housepainting and driving lessons. Perhaps they will start a chorus and sing together too. With one hundred voices in that study hall, what a chorus it could be!

There is evidence here that the new is old. When the structure on the triangle between H Street and New York Avenue had to be remodeled, the architect took care to preserve the original design of the building that had been a landmark for so long. Inside, there had to be elevators because the only place to expand was up, but from the outside people could tell by the overall shape that it was still the church. The same church where Lincoln had worshiped and dropped by on Wednesday nights for prayer when he could spare the time. He would slip quietly in and out of an adjacent room without being seen, but the door was left open so that he could hear. How did they know he ever came? Two small boys attending the meeting one night saw his profile through the frosted window between the rooms and followed him when the profile disappeared. They followed his tracks in the snow, trotting to keep up with his stride, and when the President reached the White House gates, he turned and said "Thank you, boys, for the escort."

I think he would have chuckled that summer when the

Community Club at the church tried something new, a vacation school for all children of whatever color. I think he would have smiled to see them dramatize the entrance of the ancient Hebrews into the Temple, a Japanese-American boy leading the procession as "priest," and all chanting the twenty-fourth psalm, a "Song of Ascents":

> Fling wide the gates,
>   open the ancient doors,
>   and the great king will come in!
>   Psalm 24:9, TODAY'S ENGLISH VERSION

In general the changes here have been toward informality. There is an early service every Sunday morning designed for families, some of whom gather around the piano before the service to sing hymns together, and the Children's Choir, drawn from the first six grades, often sings at this service. Since many of the children live some distance from the church, the weekly rehearsal is held after church school during the second service. Currently they are learning "The Rebel," a carol for Lent." Other favorites by Avery and Marsh are "Thank You, Thank You" and "Hey! Hey!"

Teenagers sing contemporary music with guitars and percussion, young adults gather during the week for a pot-luck supper and sing or play their instruments afterward. Between the Sunday morning services there is a coffee hour, and from time to time musical innovations are tried at the eleven o'clock service as well as at the early one. The Adult Choir has presented *Missa Criola* with a variety of instruments, including an amplified harpsichord. On Palm Sunday "Comfort Ye My People" from *Messiah* was sung back-to-back so to speak, with "Prepare Ye the Way" from *Godspell*. At the sacrament of the Lord's Supper in October, the entire congregation participated in singing

Schubert's *Mass in F.* Individual copies of the score and
liturgy had been reproduced for each person to follow.
The music is simple and easy to read, and at the early
service the choir members sat among the parents and
children and sang along with them.

Again, when the Christian home was honored in a
special service at eleven o'clock one morning, the choir
sang "Hymn of Praise" by Felix Mendelsohn:

All men, all things, all that has life and breath, sing to the
Lord . . . in joyful song extol Him.

With the complete text of the words given to the congregation that day, was this introduction, written by Edward
Clark, a member of the choir, and used here by permission:

The singing of what has been called Mendelssohn's Second
Symphony is today dedicated to the glory of God and in
honor of the Christian home.

In recent years, the American family has endured a time
of extreme crises, with an increase in divorce and with the
wedding ceremony often following only after a young
couple has established itself in home life. Through this time
of trial, the validity of home life in our country has continued to be proven, as has its adaptability.

The Christian way broadens our understanding of ourselves
and of others and teaches gentleness and kindness to all.
With God's help may we each tread softly through this
world, remembering that we tread among the dreams of
those we love and whose lives we share.

When the winds of change blow up a storm, the members of this church have dramatic reminders that God has
cared for them in the past. They see the banners that
symbolize the stability and the movement of their faith,
they see the Cross of Christ, the Bible brought in and

opened as the first act in the liturgy. They recall those who
have served as ministers, musicians, custodians, and they
think of Lincoln, whose presence is also felt. In these and
other ways they remember who they are, and at what a
price. But through the years many people here, as in other
churches, have come to realize that this is not enough. One
must keep on asking that second crucial question: "How
am I to live?" "What am I to do?" The answer may vary
for each person, but here as everywhere those who take the
question seriously discover that if the march is to go on,
they must give themselves in the context of today. Youth
who take the Jesus road may discover that the newest
things in life are as old as God, and their elders, who
thought they would know Jesus anywhere, may be astonished to see him in a teenager. In this way, in the
twinkling of an eye, all things are made new.

In Cleveland, at the end of World War II, when Japanese-Americans were relocating after their internment,
the following conversation took place in a committee
meeting at Calvary Presbyterian Church:

"I hear they're coming."

"Who?" asked the minister.

"The Japs."

"Well?"

"What if they come to church?"

The minister's reply was brief but firm: "Are we a
Christian church or aren't we?"

The Japanese-Americans did come, and some of them
became members of the church and made a gracious contribution to the life of both the church and the community.

This was the first step toward multiracial membership
for this aristocratic old church built to last, woodwork
solid maple, windows by Tiffany. Further steps came
gradually at first. There was time to grow in those days,
or so the people thought.

As lawns on Euclid Avenue became used-car lots, and the homes on side streets, rooming houses, professional people began moving out and blue-collar workers moving in. There was talk of the "black tide" coming, and churches began their exodus. The people at Calvary decided to take the risk and stay. One member went to a synod summer school to study "race," and came home seeing people differently. Others began climbing tenement stairs to make a friendly call. The minister, Dr. John Bruére at that time, stopped by school playgrounds to chat with children and in bars to visit with whoever might be there. Electronic chimes were installed in the tower and rang out for worship Sunday morning or to celebrate a victory by the Cleveland Indians. A bus was chartered for a picnic after church service, and people were encouraged to come to church in blue jeans even though they might be ushers! Truckdrivers coming off duty helped load the portable organ on the bus, and off to the country went a changing church to romp and sing and share each other's sandwiches.

But as now and then a Negro ventured in on Sunday morning to hear the music or the sermon—which was purposely kept to twenty minutes—a few people in the pews grew restless. Annie Cutter saw the shadow and had a conversation with the ushers. She was president of the Women's Guild, lived in the socially proper Heights, and was a charming seventy-five. The ushers listened.

"If you have trouble seating anyone," she said quite casually, "please feel free to bring them to my pew." They did, and it began to make a difference.

About this time there was a potluck supper called "International Smorgasbord." There were exotic dishes representing the national origins of the members, and a wall-sized map of the world on which the members put red tacks in the countries of their ancestors. Everybody comes from somewhere else, everybody is different if you go back far enough. A young woman from a "black" church

who had toured professionally in a black *Carmen* choreographed the hymn "Faith of Our Fathers" and danced it
with a friend while everybody sang the words. Faith? Yes,
"living still."

A community Christmas party was planned next. Somehow a cart and horse were found and driven up and down
the avenue with a trumpet and a poster inviting all to
"Come Sing with Us on Christmas Eve." And many did.
There was a crèche on the "porch," a choir on the steps
singing carols in the falling snow, and the minister reading
THE STORY against the traffic on the busy corner. People stopped to listen and to sing. They followed the choir
into the garden, singing "O Come All Ye Faithful." There
a tall tree was lighted and people bowed their heads and
prayed silently for a peaceful world. Four hundred guests
filed into the warm gymnasium for pie and coffee brought
over by the owners of the restaurants and bars nearby who
then stayed to share the fun. There was a Santa Claus with
presents for the children.

Things moved more quickly in the community after
this. Myths about property values and blockbusting were
challenged and opposed. Calvary joined with St. Agnes
Church across the corner to work on building codes and
sanitation. A Saturday school was opened with games and
free lunch and a singing group that included preschool
children and teenagers, black, white, handicapped, able. A
favorite song was "He's got the Whole World in His
Hand."

Nothing anybody thought of that might help was left
undone. Showers and washing machines with driers were
installed in the basement for children from the cold-water
flats, clothes and furniture were collected for special needs,
a library was opened for use on Sundays after church. It
was an imaginative and exciting program, bringing people
in the suburbs together with people of the inner city, and

through the years a wide range of culture came to be represented among both black and white members. Things were going well at the church, but not well enough in the area as a whole.

In the summer of 1967 came the shock of bombs and major riots in the Hough area only a few blocks away. The decay had been too deep, the response by slum land-lords and others in authority too meager. Jeeps rode up the avenue with soldiers carrying bayonets, a guard was posted on the corner by the church. But inside, biracial teams met and prayed and planned and went out each day to the vacant lots of the area with a schoolbell to invite children to come and sing. There were games and crafts, too, and

HENRY C. CRAWFORD

free ice cream through the long hot summer to let children know that someone cared. Helpful gifts came in, and over five thousand children were involved. The program, which was carried on for several summers, gained national recognition as the "Tot-lots" project. From it has emerged an innovative summer Teacher-Leader program sponsored by the Jennings Foundation.

Since the death of Dr. Bruére, the young man who had been his assistant during the crisis and for several years before has been available, fortunately, to carry on and help the congregation find its way. A study group of community leaders met at Calvary with the Reverend Roger Shoup and hammered out an approach to area problems that focuses on decent housing through a project known as NOAH (Neighbors Organized for Action in Housing). It is a new concept for the area, involving architects, community consultation, and community-based capital. It has the backing of the Presbytery and the Synod and offers people at the poverty level the opportunity to rent a home, with an option to buy, that is not only livable but beautiful too. The project is directed by an interracial, interfaith group representing the Hough Area Community Council as well as Calvary and St. Agnes. Recently Emmanuel Episcopal Church has also joined the project. The distinctively new thing about it is that the churches are committed not only to promote good housing on an interracial and interfaith basis, but to demonstrate it. All the members of the Board have laid their abilities and resources on the line, as have many other members of the congregations, and real progress has been made. It has been reported in an article, "Regenesis in the Inner City," published by the Jennngs Foundation.

The word "regenesis" is appropriate. Without the early beginning, the rebirth would not have been possible. Calvary Church believes that "I am not my brother's

keeper, I am his brother," and Roger Shoup gears his
sermons to the need for human caring. A recent sermon
title was "He Ain't Heavy, He's My Brother." He has
also preached on the Holy Spirit, whose presence is real,
he believes, when traditionalists, activists, pietists, and
others who have some special point of view turn to each
other and say, "You have something that I need."

The ratio of black and white members continues at
about half of each, but in keeping with current thought,
the emphasis is not so much on integration as on the need
to enable people of whatever color to have mastery of
their own lives with dignity. Youth of the suburbs continue to meet those of the inner city in the youth program
which now includes counseling on matters all the way
from drugs to college scholarships. There is also an opportunity to earn money by working on the youth staff.
In music, various traditions are welcome in the choir,
which includes children from the fourth through the
seventh grades, and there is an enthusiastic new Bell
Choir.

The members of the church know there are many new
problems to be solved before their dream for decency in
the inner city is complete, but faith in their commitment
is firm as they sing their favorite songs: "The Real Thing,"
"Put Your Hand in the Hand," "The Wedding Banquet,"
"The One Lost Sheep," "Amazing Grace," and "God
Goin' to Separate the Wheat from the Tares."

The story of Riverside Church in New York City is too
well known to need retelling in this chapter on music and
change: how Harry Emerson Fosdick would not accept
the pastorate at the "cathedral" on the Hudson unless it
was open to all races . . . how the church accepted the
mission to offer both a personal and a social gospel as expressed in the hymn written by Dr. Fosdick and sung at
the opening service: "God of Grace and God of Glory."

Many of the words are as relevant today as they must have been then. Since then this church has weathered changes in the neighborhood which have brought ever greater need and less money to meet it, yet the church has increased its concern for people, adding to its staff a minister for Urban Affairs and instituting a Metropolitan Mission study to emphasize that Christians do not change the world by withdrawing from it.

And the music continues. The entire service one Sunday morning involved both adults and children in a Festival of Hymns for which the sermon title was "Singing the Faith." And although there are now three choirs for youth and children, and two bell choirs, not to mention the Adult Choir, the congregation participated in all the singing except for one or two special arrangements. The younger choirs give two concerts a year, a sacred concert in the winter, a secular one in the spring. Not long ago the Youth Choir presented *Spoon River Anthology* to a full house. Change and revision are in the air, but the key words are "joy" and "hope"—spelled out on the children's balloons on Easter morning and in a lively youth parade one Sunday afternoon. "Whispering hope" may have been a welcome sound in the good old days, but not now. Hope and joy need to be shouted, and there is no call to be timid. We have the greatest news in the world to share.

The Riverside Youth Choir, joining with another from Westfield, New Jersey, did just that when they sang *The Great Parade* by Avery and Marsh with fourteen pieces of brass—enough to rattle the Gothic vaulting if it had not been so well built. They paraded around the sanctuary and continued outdoors with a colorful dancing clown to lead them. "I want to join the great parade, I want to join the happy caravan, of God's people, God's own people, marching round the world. There are people of all times

and places, people of all kinds and races, and here am I,
here am I, here am I." [3] Alleluia, Christ is risen!

> When you least expect Him
> He'll be there
> Read the morning headlines with a prayer.
> You'll be surprised
> What events He uses, what
> People He chooses to
> Show us His way.
>
> That's how it is
> Thru all time and hist'ry
> He is there
> And He's here today.[4]

In Port Jervis, where the Delaware valley is rimmed by
mountains, changes have been many and history colorful,
including Indians and Dutch settlers, coal barges on the
D and H Canal, the coming of the Erie. The sad decline
of the railroad with the coming of other kinds of transport
is told like it was, in a song:

> Port Jervis was a RAILROAD TOWN
> *A click and a clack on a busy track.*
> And trains went through the clock around
> *A click and a clack on a busy track.*
> Train men gathered every day
> Over drinks you'd hear them say
> Railroads, boys, are here to stay.
> Look around
> RAILROAD TOWN.

The pride of the town in their "wondrous noise" is told:

[3] © 1971, Richard K. Avery and Donald S. Marsh. *The Great Parade.*
Used by permission.
[4] © 1972, Richard K. Avery and Donald Marsh, in *Songs for the
Easter People.* Used by permission.

the "shouting of the railroad boys," the "breathing sounds
an engine makes, sounds of wheel, sounds of brakes, the
pounding in of railroad stakes."

> But one day trucks and buses came
> *A click and a clack on a busy track.*
> And railroad towns were not the same.
> *A click and a clack on a busy track.*
> The days were numbered train men knew,
> Bosses did what they had to do,
> They cut the schedules, cut the crew.
> Look around!
> RAILROAD TOWN.

The station started to decline, the trains were "two a day
instead of nine," the click and the clack were on a *lonely*
track. Few the signal lights, gone the roundhouse, gone the
sights of the town.

> One day I'm gonna meet the Lord,
> *A click and a clack on a lonely track,*
> When He calls the final "All aboard!"
> *A click and a clack on a lonely track.*
> Then bury me and let me lie
> Where children waved as trains went by.
> Mark my grave with a railroad tie
> From the town,
> RAILROAD TOWN.[5]

Into this atmosphere of nostalgia and depression came a
new factor, the significance of which was unrecognized
at the time by anyone, least of all those most closely involved. Richard Avery came to the First Presbyterian
Church as pastor, having just graduated with a B.D.
degree from Union Theological Seminary in New York.

---

[5] © 1964, Don Marsh, "Railroad Town." Used by permission.

A year or so later Donald Marsh came to direct the choir. He holds an M.A. degree in music, art, and drama from the University of Houston and has had seventeen years of show business in New York City in music, drama, choreography and directing concerts. Both he and Richard Avery sing, and they discovered they could also write music that moved people. At first it was the children, but as the girls and boys shared their enthusiasm for the new songs with the congregation, they caught on there too until even the older members missed them if only traditional hymns were sung.

During these days business was leaving town instead of coming in, but all unsuspected, a new venture as small as a mustard seed was in the making and music was the cause of it. Beginning in the basement of the manse, Proclamation Productions with a part-time staff of one high school student after hours, the minister in his spare time, and the choir director in his, were preparing to publish some of their songs: *Hymns Hot and Carols Cool.* In less than two years demand for the songbook was too much to handle. The seed had grown into a spreading tree, and in 1970 Proclamation Productions opened a new home in the house next door to the church. The remodeling process had given months of welcome work to electricians, plumbers, heating experts and painters, and the community was invited to come and celebrate. On the night of the Open House, lights streamed through the windows of this one-time funeral parlor and there was the sound of music: "Hosanna, Hallelujah! Sing we loud and clear, Hosanna, Hallelujah! Jesus Christ is here!" It was one of the songs in the new book and was being sung in person by the same quartet that had recorded it, the Vanguard Singers, all members of the church fellowship.

On the porch, celebrants were welcomed by young people presiding at a punch bowl, and inside they passed through the rooms, delighted with the transformation of the old place. Everything was new and modern except the two original fireplaces whose quaint marble mantels spoke up—nonverbally of course! "We stand for continuity in a changing world and you must admit we too have charm."

As people came and went, greeting friends, listening to music, asking questions about the pictures and other art objects, reading the new songs framed and hanging in the entrance hall, a mood of joy and exaltation pervaded the old rooms made new.

One day not long after this, I asked Kathy, who was ten at the time, what she liked about our church. She was so irrepressibly alive that her answer had to be real: "Wow!" she said, "the SONGS, that's what. The SONGS!" She lives in the country, but manages to make it to Youth Choir rehearsals. Who would want to miss singing a calypso carol, or shouting the modern equivalent of "Hallelujah" now and then: "Hooray for God!"

Since then the Proclamation songs have been carried to twenty-five states through the workshops in creative worship conducted by the Avery and Marsh team, sometimes affectionately referred to as the "Rodgers and Hammerstein of church music." We are a small church in numbers, but almost every Sunday visitors from close by or far away come to worship with us. The long-distance record is still held by a young churchman from Australia who carried some of the songs back to the folks at home where they sing them with us now halfway around the world. Marabelle Taylor says that the people in her village in the Cameroon enjoy listening to the recording of *Hymns Hot and Carols Cool* and that she is going to translate the songs into Bassa so they can sing them in their native tongue.

In keeping with the "Tidal Law" in music, which swings now in one direction, now in another, children and young people these days are also enjoying the quiet rhythm of songs from the Middle Ages or earlier, such as "Of the Father's Love Begotten." The tune is a thirteenth-century plainsong and the words are by Aurelius Prudentius (fourth century). A favorite of our Genesis Choir is "God be in My Head," with words from the *Sarum Primer* that choir boys were reciting in England as far back as 1558. The Choristers Guild has excellent study sheets on both these hymns with suggestions for use as well as background information.

At a Methodist convocation of church musicians in Lakeland, Florida, in the summer of 1973, the conference choir of young people presented a medieval Christmas service sung in Latin, with the sound of trumpets, lutes, and percussion instruments as well as an ensemble orchestra. On another occasion there, the Reverend Philip Dietrich with seven members of the same choir sang Gregorian chants, also in Latin. The last section of *Sing of Life and Faith* is rich with songs of praise in the manner of rounds, canons, and plainsong from a variety of sources including the *Genevan Psalter* and Thomas Tallis of the sixteenth century, Teleman of the seventeenth, Mozart and Haydn of the eighteenth, Cesar Franck of the nineteenth, and so on. In a similar manner but written in our own time is the song "Thank You" by Martin Schneider, also a favorite of the Genesis Choir in Port Jervis.

Recently our Crusaders Choir of teenagers sang "Morning Has Broken" by the poet Eleanor Farjeon set to an old Gaelic melody. As they sang, they dramatized very simply their awakening to a new day, their acceptance of the sunlight, and their praise for God's re-creation. It was a quiet affirmation of newness and joy from their true selves and moved the congregation deeply.

In another direction, musically, is an anthem our Adult Choir sang recently: "In the Beginning of Creation" by Daniel Pinkham. It is based on the first three verses of Genesis 1 and is written for a mixed chorus and electronic tape. Some of it (but not very much) is sung in the usual way. There are half-spoken, half-sung tones, hollow echoing syllables, and even whispers to represent chaos and darkness, wind and swirling waters. In between, or along with these, are other mysterious sounds on the tape, all leading up to the climax of "LIGHT." It was a new experience of involvement for both choir and congregation. Awe—mystery—weird but good, were among the reactions.

Whether church music will go further in this direction will be decided by the people themselves, leaders are saying. If we want it, it will be written. If we want songs in Latin, those will be created. It is good to know that renewal in worship does not have to begin with a "rock musical" or a "folk service" or some other far-out event. An article in the monthly newsletter, "In the Worship Workshop with Avery and Marsh," makes these sensible comments:

Depending on the young people for the burden of liturgical renewal is rather hypocritical and ultimately self-defeating. And communicating the idea that innovative worship consists primarily of one style of presentation is dangerous, especially when that style involves turned-up amplifiers! Renewal in worship more effectively begins when the pastor speaks and prays in natural everyday language; when the congregation is allowed to speak for itself on occasion; when the Scripture reading is literally put on its feet by uncostumed actors; or when an old hymn is sung twice, with an enthusiastic search for its meaning between the two times.

At an Open House at our church, in October, for those involved in church music, "The Magnificat," a new song by Donald Marsh, was sung as a duet in Latin. The hundred or so people present seemed open to the new or different, not as seekers after novelty, but for whatever ways will continue to make worship real. They had come

from the church across the square and from as far away as
Maine, the Middle West, and Philadelphia. John and
Helen Kemp were there from the Westminster Choir
College in Princeton, and Carlton Young, who composes
music as well as arranging and compiling it, had come from
Dallas. Many of us in our own choir were attending this
kind of conference for the first time.

Carlton Young spoke of the need to "put some mobility"
into our places of worship, and when we chose partners to
sing "We are the Church," we experienced something of
his meaning in relation to the people present and to "All
who follow Jesus, all around the world." Yes, we are the
church together.

Another good song for "mobility" is an introit we sang
on Pentecost at the Presbytery workshop:

> We're here to be happy, we're here to be moved
> We're here together to hear together the Good News.
> So weep if you want to or shout hip hooray!
> God's ready to meet you on this and every day.
> Sing halelujah, sing halelujah, sing halelujah my friend!
> God is the beginning and God is the end.[6]

On the "hallelujah" everybody clapped their wrists together
like cymbals and raised their arms high. After this song was
sung at a conference in Montreat, North Carolina, two
women said, "We didn't know religion could be so much
fun." The following year the song "Come as a Child" by
Avery and Marsh was dedicated to the women of that
conference and published in *Alive and Singing*.

A journey makes a good mobility song. Someone is on
the move, leaving the old life behind, like Abraham, or
seeking the new as the three Wise Men did, symbols of
the nations of the world. Journeys for God involve pur-

[6] © 1972, by Richard Avery and Donald S. Marsh, in *Hooray for
God*. Used by permission.

pose, faith, obedience and risk, sometimes a surprise. Moses goes to look at a bush aflame and gets an incredible assignment. Jesus goes to Jerusalem to celebrate a festival and is crucified. We have a few journey songs like "The Epiphany Carol" in *Hymns Hot and Carols Cool* or "The Trip to Bethlehem" in *Sing for Joy*, but we could use more. Journeys have a strong appeal for children, and young people enjoy "go-go" with a difference. This may be one reason why our choir now has several dismissal songs all beginning with "Go!" In Advent, the first words are: "Go tell everyone, starting with your neighbor"; in Lent, "Go and walk the way with Him."

One Sunday morning recently, our learning was related to the meaning of "Go"—the call of God to Moses to "Go tell old Pharaoh to let my people go," and God's call to us to "Go into all the world." Each of us was given a "Go" button to wear, the *O* designed to look like the world we are called to serve. The Crusaders Choir sang the spiritual "Go Down, Moses" with simple hand-and-arm movements, and at the end of the song, they stood with arms outstretched to represent the cross, God's act of re-creation.

Where will they be going on their missions of compassion and concern? Where will we go on ours? To Africa? India? Port Jervis? Next door? If we listen carefully, we will hear the music of a new world as people of every age, faith, race, and nation converge toward the promised land.

And I heard every creature in heaven, on earth, and in the world below . . . all creatures in the whole universe—and they were *singing*:
"To him who sits on the throne, and to the Lamb.
Be praise and honor, glory and might,
For ever and ever!"

Revelation 5:13
Today's English Version

Resources and Their Sources

General Bibliography

Ashton-Warner, Sylvia. *Spearpoint: Teacher in America*. New York: Knopf, 1972. Interesting commentary on the need to have dreams, p. 87.

Atwood, Ann. *My Own Rhythm*. New York: Scribners, 1973. An approach to the Japanese poetic form, haiku, with photographs in full color by the author.

Bookspan, Martin. *One Hundred One Masterpieces of Music and Their Composers*. Garden City, N.Y.: Doubleday, 1968.

Burakoff, Gerald, and Laurence Wheeler. *Music Making in the Elementary School*. New York: Hargail Music, Inc., 1968. One of the Teacher's Education Series, based on concepts of Orff and Kodaly, using a recorder, the voice, bells, and rhythm instruments.

Chase, Gilbert. *America's Music from the Pilgrims to the Present*. New York: McGraw-Hill, 1955.

Children in Community, ed. by Society of Brothers. Rifton, New York: Plough, 1963. Articles on education, with pictures that inspire renewed hope.

Coleman, Satis M. *Creative Music for Children*. New York: Putnam. Out of print, but worth trying for in a library. Practical ideas include rhythmic activity and how children can make their own instruments.

Copland, Aaron. *Copland on Music*. New York: Norton, 1963.

Davison, Archibald T. *Church Music: Illusion and Reality*. Cambridge: Harvard University Press, 1952.

Dickinson, Edward. *Music in the History of the Western Church*. New York: AMS Press, 1970. Reprint of the 1902 Scribners edition.

Ferguson, Donald N. *The Why of Music*. Minneapolis: University of Minnesota Press, 1969.

Grant, Parks. *Music for Elementary Teachers*, 2nd ed. New York: Appleton, 1960.

Kemp, Helen. *Music in Church Education with Children*. Dallas: Choristers Guild, 1970. Originally commissioned by the United Presbyterian Church for summer classes; published with its cooperation as a "syllabus" by the Choristers Guild.

Koch, Kenneth. *Wishes, Lies and Dreams: Teaching Children to Write Poetry*. New York: Chelsea House, 1970. The exciting experiment at P.S. 61 in New York City is presented by the teacher's comments and the pupils' own poetry.

Luck, James T. *Creative Music for the Classroom Teacher*. New York: Random House, 1971.

McGinley, Phyllis. *Saint Watching.* New York: Viking, 1969.

Morman, Jean Mary. *Wonder Under Your Feet.* New York: Harper & Row, 1973. Photographs with perceptive coment on the beauty of the "real" that begins under our feet. We ourselves are "in" today's art, not outside it.

Nordoff, Paul, and Clive E. Robbins. *Music Therapy in Special Education.* New York: John Day, 1971.

Roberts, Ronald. *Musical Instruments Made to Be Played.* Leicester, England: Dryad Press.

Rothmüller, Aron Marco. *The Music of the Jews.* Cranbury, N.J.: A. S. Barnes, 1960.

Routley, Erik. *Music Leadership in the Church.* Nashville: Abingdon Press, 1967. A "conversation" with his American friends by the former director of music and chaplain of Mansfield College, Oxford, now minister of a Congregational church in Edinburgh, Scotland.

Rublowski, John. *Music in America.* New York: Macmillan, 1967. From psalms and ballads of Colonial days to jazz, folk/rock, and electronic sounds. Puritans were not as dour as sometimes pictured.

Sanders, James A. *Torah and Canon.* Philadelphia: Fortress Press, 1972.

Sheehy, Emma D. *Children Discover Music and Dance.* Early Childhood Education. New York: Teachers College Press, Columbia University, 1968.

Shippen, Katherine B. and Anca Seidlova. *The Heritage of Music.* New York: Viking, 1963.

Sigmeister, Elie. *Invitation to Music.* Irvington-on-Hudson, N.Y.: Harvey House, 1961. Attractive to both children and adults.

Szabo, Helga. *The Kodály Concept of Music Education.* Oceanside N.Y.: Boosey & Hawkes, 1969. The English edition by Geoffrey Russell-Smith is accompanied by three records which provide illustrations of the different stages and techniques reviewed.

Terrence, E. Paul. *Guiding Creative Talent.* Englewood Cliffs, N.J.: Prentice-Hall, 1962.

Special Books: For Children (Young and Old!)

Allstrom, Elizabeth. *Songs Along the Way.* Nashville: Abingdon Press, 1961. Selected psalms with background comment and illustrated with vigorous woodcuts of authentic spirit.

Baldwin, Lillian. *Music for Young Listeners.* Morristown, N.J.: Silver Burdett, 1951. Excellent material on "patterns" in music.

Also life stories of a few composers, the one on Bach being of
special interest for church education.

Black, Irma Simonton. *Castle, Abbey and Town: How People
Lived in the Middle Ages.* New York: Holiday House, 1963.
Combines fiction with history; shows how the music of the
minstrels related to the customs of the period. Ages 9–12.

Clement, Jane T. *The Sparrow.* Rifton, N.Y.: Plough, 1968. Five
stories and seven poems "bound together by a sense of expec-
tancy, a belief that something new is on the way."

Ellison, Virginia H. *The Pooh Get Well Book.* New York:
Dutton, 1973. Inspired by A. A. Milne's four books about
Christopher Robin and Winnie the Pooh.

Fosdick, Harry E. *Martin Luther.* New York: Random House,
1956.

Fraser, Beatrice and Ferrin. *The Secret of the Bells.* Dallas:
Choristers Guild. A winter story about the influence of the
sound of bells on the life of a small boy who lives in a mountain
village. Any church with a handbell program will find this
especially appealing. It can be dramatized using a narrator with
singing and bell choirs.

Gough, Catherine. *Boyhoods of Great Composers.* 2 Bks. New
York: Walck, 1960–1965.

Holl, Adelaide. *Too Fat to Fly.* Champaign, Ill.: Garrard, 1973.
An elephant discovers what he *can* do. Delightful drawings by
Bill Morrison, Gr. K–3.

Macdonald, George. *The Princess and the Goblin.* New York:
Macmillan, 1957. A fairy tale containing some wisdom about
music.

Pottebaum, Gerard A. *Psalm 8 from the Voices of Children.* Little People's Paperback. Dayton: Pflaum, 1965. A prayer with an
antiphon and music to sing it in the style of a chant. Illustrated
with finger paintings.

Society of Brothers, eds. *Behold That Star.* 2nd ed. Rifton, N.Y.:
Plough, 1966. A collection of 15 Christmas stories recommended
for family reading. Gr. 2–6.

Wheeler, Opal, and Sybil Deucher. *Sebastian Bach: The Boy from
Thuringia.* New York: Dutton, 1973.

Special Books: For Crafts

Laliberte, Norman, and Sterling McIlhaney. *Banners and Hang-
ings: Design and Construction.* New York: Van Nostrand Rein-
hold, 1966.

Norbeck, Oscar V. *Book of Indian Life Crafts.* New York: Tower
Publications, 1970. Paperback reprint of 1968 ed. A handbook

of North American Indian crafts; includes sources-of-supplies
listing.
The Family Creative Workshop. New York and Amsterdam:
Plenary Publications International, Inc., 1974. A comprehensive
set of books, covering traditional and contemporary crafts.

See also "Choir Aids," "Worship Aids," for other special books.

Poetry: For Rhythm, Fun, Joy

Blishen, Edward. *Oxford Book of Poetry for Children*. New
York: Franklin Watts, 1964. Gr. K–3.
Brewton, Sara and John E. *Birthday Candles Burning Bright*. New
York: Macmillan, 1960. Gr. 4–6.
Cole, William. *Poems for Seasons and Celebrations*. New York:
World, 1961.
Eastwick, Ivy O. *In and Out the Windows*. Rifton, N.Y.: Plough,
1969. Twenty happy poems set to music by Marlys Swinger as
happy songs, all in the same book; illustrations by Gillian Barth
give an extra touch of magic.
Lewis, Richard, compiler. *The Wind and the Rain: Children's
Poems*, illus. with photographs by Helen Butterfield. New York:
Simon and Schuster, 1968.
Meyers, Garry Cleveland. *Wishes*. Old Tappan, N.J.: Hewitt
House, 1969. Children will recognize themselves in both poems
and illustrations in this collection produced with the coopera-
tion of Highlights for Children, Inc.
Moore, Lillian. *Catch Your Breath*. Champaign, Ill.: Garrard, 1973.
A book of shivery poems.
O'Neil, Mary. *Hailstones and Halibut Bones*. Garden City, N.Y.:
Doubleday, 1973.
Patterson, Lillie. *Poetry for Spring*. Champaign, Ill.: Garrard,
1973.
Read, Sir Herbert, ed. *This Way Delight*. New York: Pantheon,
1956.

Poetry: For Humor

Berg, Jean Horton. *Miss Tessie Tate*. Philadelphia: Westminster
Press, 1967. A story in rhymed couplets about a jolly old lady
who practices roller skating from morning till night. Joyous
funny pictures by Lee DeGroot.
DeRegniers, Beatrice. *Something Special*. New York: Harcourt,
1958.

Nash, Ogden. *The Moon Is Shining Bright As Day*. Philadelphia:
Lippincott, 1953.
Palazzo, Tony, compiler and illus. *Edward Lear's Nonsense Book*.
Garden City: Doubleday, 1956.
Petersen, Isobel. *The First Book of Poetry*. New York: Franklin
Watts, 1954. Includes "Gordon Gustavus Gore" and "Eletele-
phony," as well as poems by A. A. Milne, Eleanor Farjeon, Rose
Fyleman, Robert Louis Stevenson.
Starbird, Kaye. *Don't Ever Cross a Crocodile*. Philadelphia: Lip-
pincott, 1963. Includes "Tuesday I Was Ten" and "Measles."

See also "Recordings."

Songbooks

A New Now: A Youth Folk Hymnal. Carol Stream, Ill.: Hope
Publishing Co., 1971.
Avery, Richard, and Donald Marsh. *Alive and Singing*. Port Jer-
vis, N.Y.: Proclamation Productions, 1971. Includes "He's
Alive"; "O God, O Son of God"; "Shine, Star!"; "What Makes
the Wind Blow?"; "Mission Possible," etc.
————. Book #6. Port Jervis, N.Y.: Proclamation Productions, 1974.
Includes "Different is Beautiful."
————. *Hymns Hot and Carols Cool*. Port Jervis, N.Y.: Proclama-
tion Productions, 1967. Includes "Hey! Hey! Anybody Listen-
ing?'; "Mary, Mary"; "Gloria"; "Doxology"; "He Was a Rebel,"
etc. (Record available.)
————. *More, More, More*. Port Jervis, N.Y.: Proclamation Produc-
tions, 1970. Includes "Born Again"; "I Wonder Why"; "O Let's
Get On"; "Happy Birthday (to the church)"; "Goodbye," etc.
————. *Songs for the Easter People*. Port Jervis, N.Y.: Proclama-
tion Productions, 1972. Includes "When You Least Expect
Him"; "Here He Comes"; "Blood"; "We Are the Church";
"Every Morning Is Easter Morning," etc.
————. *Songs for the Search*. Port Jervis, N.Y.: Proclamation Pro-
ductions, 1973. Includes "Love Them Now"; "My Kind of
Music"; "Thank You, Lord"; "Explorer," etc.
Bacon, Denise, arranger. *Let's Sing Together*. Wellesley Hills,
Mass.: Kodály Musical Training Institute, 1971. Songs from
Mother Goose and others, set to music according to the Kodály
concept. For 3-, 4-, and 5-year-olds, in nursery schools, day
care centers, or home.
Crain, Margaret L., compiler. *Kindergarten Songs and Rhythms*.
Valley Forge, Pa.: Judson Press. (Record available.)

———, compiler. *Nursery Songs and Rhythms.* Valley Forge, Pa.: Judson Press. For 2- and 3-year-olds at home or church. (Record available.)

Curry, W. Lawrence, ed. *Hymnal for Juniors: In Worship and Study.* Philadelphia: Westminster Press, 1966.

Curry, Lawrence *et al.*, eds. *Songs and Hymns for Primary Children.* Philadelphia: Westminster Press, 1963.

———, eds. *Songs for Early Childhood: At Church and Home.* Philadelphia: Westminster Press, 1958.

Folk Encounter. Carol Stream, Ill.: Hope Publishing Co., 1973. "New music" for Christians.

Lullabies and Night Songs, ed. by William Engvick; music by Alec Wilder; pictures by Maurice Sendak. New York: Harper & Row, 1965. The rollicking songs are not strictly lullabies, but are intended to end the day "with laughter and delight."

McNeil, Margaret Crain, compiler. *Come Sing with Me.* Valley Forge, Pa.: Judson .Press, 1972. For church school, family, nursery school, day-care centers.

Mealy, Norman and Margaret, compilers and eds. *Sing for Joy: A Songbook for Young Children.* New York: Seabury Press, 1961. For church school, family, nursery school, day-care centers.

Miller, Max B., and Louise C. Drew, eds. *Sing of Life and Faith.* Philadelphia: United Church Press, 1969.

Paterson, James, and James Ross, eds. *Songs for the Seventies.* Great Yarmouth, England: Galliard, 1972. Fifty-two new hymns and songs for the Church of Scotland and Christians everywhere.

Pooler, Marie. *A Child Sings.* Minneapolis: Augsburg Publishing House. Stresses "walking the beat" while singing.

Pre-school Songs for the Autoharp. Nashville: Broadman Press.

Rogers, Fred. *Mr. Rogers' Songbook.* New York: Random House, 1970. Known through the NET-TV series, "Mr. Rogers' Neighborhood." For young children. (Record available.)

Routley, Erik, and Reginald Barret-Ayres, eds. *New Songs for the Church.* Bk. 1. Great Yarmouth, England: Galliard, 1969. Psalms, children's songs, ballads, hymns.

Sacred Canons, or Rounds from Ancient Times. Delaware, O.: Cooperative Recreation Service, Inc.

Smith, Peter, ed. *Faith, Folk and Nativity.* Great Yarmouth, England: Galliard, 1968. Melody line and guitar chords. Includes "Every Star Shall Sing a Carol"; "Standing in the Rain"; "Lament of an Old Age Pensioner"; "Oh, Who Would Be a Shepherd Boy?" etc.

———, ed. *New Orbit.* Great Yarmouth, England: Galliard. Songs and hymns for "under elevens." Editions with or without music.

Swann, Donald. *Sing Around the Year*. Great Yarmouth, England: Galliard. (Record available.)

Swinger, Marlys, arranger. *Sing Through the Day*, ed. by Society of Brothers. Rifton, N.Y.: Plough, 1968. Ninety songs for younger children.

————, arranger. *Sing Through the Seasons*, ed. by Society of Brothers; illus. by Moneil, Susanna, and Biene. Rifton, N.Y.: Plough. Ninety-nine songs for children. (Record available.)

Thomas, Edith Lovell, compiler. *The Whole World Singing*. New York: Friendship Press, 1950.

Wigwam. Delaware, O.: Cooperative Recreation Service, Inc. Ten songs form the Iroquois, Ottawa, and Chippewa Indians.

Young, Carlton, compiler. *The Genesis Songbook*. Chicago: Agape Press, 1973. Songs for "getting it all together," editions for guitar or with piano accompaniment.

See also "Choir Aids," "Cantatas," "Recordings," "Worship Aids."

Choir Aids: From the Choristers Guild

The following choral aids, a descriptive catalogue of these and all other resources available from the Choristers Guild, as well as Guild membership information may be obtained by addressing the Choristers Guild, P.O. Box 38188, Dallas, Tex. 75238.

Christensen, Helga. *Better Choir Singing*, trans. by Paulette Moeller. A textbook on choral work, translated from the Danish.

Choristers Guild Letter. Published monthly, September through June, and distributed to Choristers Guild members, these informal newsletters deal with choir organization, rehearsal planning, musicianship, hymn learning, review of new music, news of children's and youth choirs, workshops, seminars, and much more.

Gallagher, Melvin L. *Notes of Music*. A manual on methods of teaching the language of music. The author has had outstanding success in teaching young children by using a large music staff on the floor and notes and rests on various-sized blocks. Children advance from floor to blackboard to printed page.

Hymn Study Series. Seventy-six creative and informative studies for use in children's choirs. Each study is on a separate sheet and contains both the hymn and background material as well as suggested activity. Studies may be ordered separately by name and number, from the Choristers Guild catalogue.

Jacobs, Ruth K. *The Successful Children's Choir*. A book of techniques for handling children's voices and organizing choirs; includes suggested choral material and morale-building methods.

Tufts, Nancy Poor. *The Children's Choir*. Beginning with the primary choir, the book continues through the youth choir and the bell choir and covers both the small congregation and the large multiple-choir program.

Cantatas

Barefoot School. Music by Robert Graham. Choristers Guild. This cantata for children's choir, a teacher (soprano), and a narrator was composed to honor the coming of missionaries to Hawaii in 1820. The melodies are authentic ones used by missionaries in the schools.

Christmas in Holland. By Helen Kemp. Choristers Guild. A miniature play for children's choir, narrator, and pantomime group, it contains seven authentic Sinterklaas and Christmas carols arranged for junior-age singers.

Godsend. By Richard Avery and Donald Marsh. Philadelphia: Fortress Press, 1974. A celebration for Advent written for adult choirs and older youth.

Joseph and the Amazing Technicolor Dreamcoat. Music by Andrew Lloyd; words by Tim Rice. Belwin Mills, Publisher.

100% Chance of Rain. By Walter S. Horsley. Choristers Guild. This adaptation of the story of Noah has simple, singable melodies with childlike humor.

The Christmas Jazz. By Lloyd and Chappell. England: Clarabella Music Ltd. The Bethlehem story seen through the eyes of the animals is presented with both reverence and fun. One of a series of cantatas based on biblical stories (including Goliath, Jericho, the Red Sea, the Prodigal Son, and others), it was first presented by school children on London Weekend Television in 1971.

The Shepherd's Pipe. Poems by Johannes Gick; music by Marlys Swinger. Plough (The Society of Brothers). This cantata for children's voices or youth choir "has as its center the fact of Christmas, but all of the voices that speak through it are for every day and every time." (Record available.)

The Song of Caedmon. Music by Donald Swann; words by Arthur Scholey. Galliard. The story of the seventh-century lay brother at the Abbey of Whitby and the miracle of God's gift to him of poetry and song is simply told. The music is scored for piano, recorder, and bells, but can be performed to suit available resources. Junior- and junior high-age children may combine to perform this cantata. (Record available.)

This Is the Story of Bontzye Shweig. Music by Donald Swann; words by Leslie Paul. Galliard. The possibilities for producing this enduring legend from Yiddish folklore are flexible: with or without a children's choir, as a concert piece, or costumed with mime and pageantry.

We Have a King. By Shirley Whitecotton. Choristers Guild. Plainsong and traditional melodies are used, as well as original themes, in this short Easter cantata written especially with children's voices in mind.

Recordings

HYMNS, SONGS, CAROLS

A Song for All Seasons. Proclamation Productions. Avery and Marsh songs, presented by Dick and Don and Their Singing Friends from Princeton, include "Come As a Child"; "My Kind of Music"; "I Come Tired"; "Love Them Now," etc.

Boggs Academy Acapella Chorus. Mark Custom Records (stereo MC 6721). C. W. Francis, director; Stanley Jackson, student director.

Chapel Choir in a Sacred Concert, vol. 7. Hope College. Directed by Robert W. Cavanaugh, the choir sings "O Clap Your Hands" (Ralph Vaughn Williams); "Jesus and the Traders" (Zoltan Kodály); "If Ye Love Me" (Daniel Pinkham); "Magnificat" (Charles Theodore Pachelbel), and other sacred songs.

Faith, Folk and Nativity. Galliard. A companion to the songbook of the same title edited by Peter Smith presents joyous songs to celebrate joyous occasions.

Hymns Hot and Carols Cool. Proclamation Productions. The Vanguard Singers present songs for the church year from the Avery and Marsh songbook of the same name, including "Hey! Hey! Anybody Listening?"; "Take Time"; "Mary, Mary"; "Hosanna, Hallelujah"; "Thank You, Thank You," etc.

Kindergarten Songs and Rhythms. Judson Press. A companion to the songbook of the same name compiled by Margaret L. Crain, but sold separately, this is a sing-along-and-do teaching record.

Mr. Rogers' Songbook. Columbia Records. NET-TV's Fred Rogers's ("Mr. Rogers' Neighborhood") songs from his songbook of the same name. If unavailable from local record stores, order from Small World Enterprises, Inc., 4716, Ellsworth Ave., Pittsburgh, Pa. 15213.

Nursery Songs and Rhythms. Judson Press. A companion to the

songbook of the same name compiled by Margaret L. Crain, but
sold separately, this is another sing-along-and-do teaching record, this one designed for 2- and 3-year-olds at home or church.
Sing Around the Year. Galliard. Selections from Galliard's companion book of Donald Swann's songs are presented by Swann
with the girls of Mayfield School and the boys of Westminster
School, England, and feature new carols for children and their
parents, including rounds and canticles.
Sing Through the Seasons. Plough. Sold separately or together
with its companion book of the same name (Marlys Swinger,
arranger, edited by Society of Brothers), this recording fea-
tures "Sing a Song of Spring"; "Lippity-Lop"; "Jack-o-Lan-
tern"; "Icicles," among other selections.
You'll Sing a Song and I'll Sing a Song. Ella Jenkins. Folkways
Records.

CANTATAS

The Shepherd's Pipe: Songs of the Holy Night. Plough. Marlys
Swinger's Christmas cantata is sung by 55 children, grades 4–12.
The Song of Caedmon. Galliard (4014). Donald Swann and school
children present his and Arthur Scholey's cantata based on the
story of God's gift of poetry and song to a lay brother of the
seventh century at the Abbey of Whitby.

MUSIC FROM OUR CHRISTIAN HERITAGE

Bach. *The Eight Little Preludes and Fugues.* Columbia Records
(ML-5978). E. Power Biggs plays the classical organs of Europe.
Bach, Haydn, and others. *An 18th Century Concert.* Vanguard
BG-589). Includes Corelli's "Christmas Concerto," Haydn's
"Toy Symphony," and Bach's "Jesu, Joy of Man's Desiring."
Beethoven. *Symphony No. 9 in D Minor.* Any available record-
ing. The last movement contains the "Ode to Joy" on which is
based the hymn "Joyful, Joyful, We Adore Thee."
Gregorian Chant: *Missa De Angelis* and *Missa Cum Jubilo.* Gre-
gorian Institutes of America (PX-2).
Music of the Middle Ages. Haydn Society Records (HSE-9100).
Palestrina. *Missa Papae Marcelli.* Deutsche Grammophon/Archive
(198182).

MUSIC OF INTERCULTURAL INFLUENCE

Leonard Bernstein. *Jeremiah Symphony.* Columbia Records (MS-
6303). The two sources of genuine Hebraic music—cantillation

of the Bible and liturgical chant of the synagogue—are reflected
in the solemnity and reverence of this work; modern trends in
music are mirrored in the dancelike, almost jazzy rhythms that
appear from time to time.

Missa Luba. Philips (PCC-606). None of the music of this mass is
written. It is sung in pure Congolese style by a choir of 45 boys
and 15 teachers organized by Fr. Guido Haazen, a white priest
from Belgium, who came to the Congo to learn as well as teach.
While the mass is arranged in the familiar Kyrie, Gloria, Credo,
and so on, the music is without any Western influence, but re-
flects the rhythms of the Congo. For music of North American
Indians, write to Folkways Records, New York.

POETRY

A Child's Garden of Verses. Caedmon Records. Robert Louis
Stevenson's poems recorded by Judith Anderson. G. 2–5.

Carl Sandburg's Poems for Children. Caedmon Records. Recorded
by Sandburg. Gr. 4–6.

Miracles. Caedmon Records. The original poetry of children ages
5–13, recorded by Julie Harris and Roddy McDowell. Gr.
K–8.

Mother Goose. Caedmon Records. Recorded by Cyril Ritchard,
Celeste Holm, and Boris Karloff. Gr. K–1.

Ogden Nash Reads Ogden Nash. Eye Gate House. Gr. 4–8.

Poetry for Me. Follett Corp. Gr. K–6.

Poet's Gold. RCA Victor Records. Recorded by Helen Hayes,
Raymond Massey, and Thomas Mitchell. Gr. 4–8.

Robert Frost Reads Robert Frost. Eye Gate House. Gr. 3–8.

Films

Children Dance. 14 min. Extension Media Center. Boys and girls
from kindergarten through third grade improvise feeling,
moods, ideas, in dance in this film that demonstrates how dance
can be introduced by nonspecialist teachers.

Dance Your Own Way. 10 min./color. BFA Educational Media.
Designed to motivate free self-expression to music, the film
shows children dancing, whirling, and moving rhythmically.

Orff Musical Instruments. For information about films on using
Orff instruments write to Swank Motion Pictures, 201 Jefferson Ave., St. Louis, Mo. 63103.

Poetry for Me. 14 min. Grover-Jennings. Gr. 1–6.

The Family—A Sharing Together. Sponsored by Reformed

Church of America. Rental from Travarca, P.O. Box 247, Grandville, Mich. 49418. Experiences are real, not sentimental, as parents and children have fun learning, growing, making things. The four songs featured are by Avery and Marsh and were especially commissioned for this film. The one about "The Holy Spirit and Elmer's Glue" will appeal to any group that makes things together, but especially to a family. A booklet of the four songs may be ordered from Proclamation Productions, Orange Square, Port Jervis, N.Y. 12771.

Your Voice. 11 min. Encyclopaedia Britannica Films. Animated drawings illustrate the use of the voice in speaking and singing.

Filmstrips

Introduction to Music Readings. Filmstrip/record/teacher's guide. Educational Audio-Visual, Inc. In this presentation children learn the basic elements of music reading through rhythmic activities, singing, playing simple melody instruments.

Music and Art: Our Common Heritage. Educational Audio-Visual, Inc. Will acquaint elementary-age children with the relationship that music and art bear to other activities. A booklet (included) gives ideas for correlating activity.

Singing Games

Best Singing Games. By Edgar S. Bley. Sterling Publishing Co. For children of all ages.

Listen! and Help Tell The Story. By Bernice Carlson. Nashville, Tn.: Abingdon Press. Songs and finger play for pre-school ages.

Sing, Children, Sing. Chappell & Co. Songs, dances, and singing games of many lands and peoples; published by arrangement with UNICEF.

Worship Aids

Around the Table "Family Carol Sing." Choristers Guild. A booklet of 17 carols with Scripture arranged in madrigal-type service by Mable Boyter.

Banner Patterns. Proclamation Productions. Eight patterns for banners representing elements of the Christian faith, beginning with the Nicene Creed, three of which relate especially to the reformed and Presbyterian traditions. Includes a festival service of worship.

Bitgood, Roberta, ed. *Altogether Joyfully Sing*. Choristers Guild. Worship responses for juiors and others.

Bosch, Paul. *Worship Work Bench*. Lutheran Church Council. Originally prepared for circulation among colleges, this comprehensive look at both traditional and contemporary worship by the Reverend Mr. Bosch includes practical suggestions for worship.

Carroll, James. *Wonder and Worship*. Paulist/Newman Press. Fr. Carroll's stories for celebration, told in the style of fairy tales, are useful for reading alone, in the family, in a prayer group, and/or in a Eucharistic setting.

Christ Is Risen. Multimedia Packet. John and Mary Harrell. This Resurrection celebration for children of grades 1–4 includes a filmstrip (in color), a record for singing, listening, movement (as well as narration), a utilization guide, and directions for creating an experience of rejoicing.

Cries for Help. Proclamation Productions. An easy-to-stage four-part round (for soloists or choirs) about human need, presented in the style of street vendors' cries, as featured in the motion picture *Any Milk Today?*

Definition of Passion. Filmstrips; recorded narration and music. John and Mary Harrell. A presentation for adults that brings into relationship great paintings of Christ's Passion and memorable news photographs of recent years. Two projectors and two screens are required. The presentation concludes with washes of color over the two screens and the spontaneous music of Christopher Tree, who improvises on 150 gongs, bells, and templehorns. With more limited objectives, it may be used with senior and junior highs.

Go! Proclamation Productions. Six choral benedictions to send the congregation forth with purpose around the church year.

Hooray for God. Proclamation Productions. Service music for choirs: introits, amens, dismissals.

In the Worship Workshop with Avery and Marsh. C.S.S. Publishing Co. A monthly newsletter with creative ideas fresh from the proving ground of a Port Jervis, N.Y., church. (NOTE: "A Sample Service of Hymns" from the Workshop may be found at the end of this section on "Worship Aids.")

Love, O Love. Proclamation Productions. A sermon (or program) in song and improvised scenes about the need for love in daily relationships that may be used in services, conferences, youth and adult groups.

Young Carlton. *New Music for the Church*. Agape Press. Fourteen articles and responses for congregation and choir.

Love Them Now. Proclamation Productions. A sermon in song
and improvised scenes, this is a program for all ages to share,
with laughs and tears.

Sloyan, Virginia, and Gabe Huck. *Children's Liturgies.* Liturgical
Conference. A book to involve children in imaginative worship
celebrations they can understand and enjoy.

The Fire and the Wind. Multimedia Packet. John and Mary Harrell. This inquiry into the meaning of Pentecost for Christians
today includes a filmstrip, a record, a poem-narration, a study
paper on the Holy Spirit, a booklet of symbols, and a utilization guide. Gr. 6 and up.

The Great Parade. Proclamation Productions. A rousing parade
song for Christians and a festival service to involve the entire
congregation.

Zdenek, Marilee, and Marge Champion. *Catch the New Wind.*
Word, Inc. A book to inspire creative worship.

A Sample Service of Hymns*

* This hymn service is presented here by special permission of "In
the Worship Workshop with Avery and Marsh," the monthly newsletter published by C.S.S. Publishing Co. (see listing, above), from
which it is reprinted. The newsletter's introductory paragraph notes
that the outline offers "a few words to indicate possibilities for the
narration and a few ideas for the presentation of the songs. A bulletin
printed for the day need not contain more than general information
about the songs' origins—names, centuries, etc. At the top of the bulletin
or program: 'SONGS OF THE PEOPLE OF GOD' and beneath this
title somewhere: "from all kinds of people . . . from all times and
places.' "

Call to Worship: Verses from Psalm 95

Introit: "O for a Thousand Tongues"

(Sung by several soloists standing one by one among the congregation without announcement, joining on succeeding lines
of the song)

NARRATION: (in this case after the singing): We have begun
with a song from the pen of Charles Wesley, the 18th-century
writer of the words for 6,500 hymns. The hymns of Wesley,
who helped his brother John found what is now the Methodist
Church, have shaped our understanding of the faith . . .

Invocation

Songs of Celebration:

"All People That on Earth Do Dwell"
(Old Hundredth)

NARRATION: We go back to the 16th century and to Geneva, Switzerland. Louis Bourgeois wrote music for the emerging Reformation church there. William Kethe, a Scotch refugee, wrote this adaptation of the 100th Psalm for singing. This is the oldest hymn preserved from those early days of Protestant-ism . . .

"The Lord of the Dance"

NARRATION: This song combines three elements: a poetic picture from the Middle Ages of a dancing Jesus, a "Shaker" tune from early America, and the composing talent of a contemporary English song writer and performer named Sidney Carter . . . (The song might best be done by a soloist on the stanzas and the people joining on the refrain after a quick rehearsal. Use light percussion.)

"My Hope Is Built on Nothing Less"

NARRATION: A cabinet maker and reporter named Edward Mote became a Baptist minister at the age of 55 and wrote many songs to express his faith. This happy and bouncy "gospel song" is one of them . . .

Songs of Communion:

"Saviour, Like a Shepherd Lead Us"

NARRATION: These anonymous words inspired by Psalm 23 are sung to a tune by William Bradbury, a New York City music teacher and conductor . . .

"To Thee Before the Close of Day"

(In the Episcopal 1940 Hymnal)

NARRATION: This is one of the very oldest hymns still sung, with words from the 7th century and a tune from the 6th! The whole song consists of just four notes, typical of the simplicity and starkness of the music of the ancient church . . .

"When I'm Feeling Lonely"

(In *Hymns Hot and Carols Cool* [see listing under "Songbooks," above].)

(With solo stanzas sung from around the room)

NARRATION: We leap across 1,300 years for another hymn of personal communion with God, one from our own time and from the United States. Richard Avery and Donald Marsh wrote this song in response to the loneliness and the probing questions shared by members of their congregation in Port Jervis, New York . . .

"Be Still, My Soul"

NARRATION: These words are by the German poet, Katharine von Schlegel; she wrote them in the 18th century. The tune is from the majestical orchestral work "Finlandia" by the composer Jan Sibelius of Finland . . .

Songs of Challenge:

"Once to Every Man and Nation"

NARRATION: This is a century-old protest song. These words are from a poem of 1845 by Harvard professor James Russell Lowell, written to protest the war with Mexico. This tune was, in Welsh legend, said to have been washed ashore in a bottle; thus it is called "Ton-y-botel" ("Tune in a Bottle") . . .

"Turn, Turn, Turn"

(By a soloist, accompanied by guitar, with congregation invited to join on the repeated words, "Turn, turn, turn")

NARRATION: This is a song by contemporary balladeer Pete Seeger based on words from the Bible's Book of Ecclesiastes. It was one of the most popular song hits of the 1960s—a call to repentance and wisdom . . .

"God of Our Fathers"

NARRATION: Daniel C. Roberts, an Episcopal rector in Vermont, wrote the words of this hymn for our nation's centennial in

1876. A prayer for our nation's future, it is still relevant as we approach a second centennial in 1976. The tune is by George Warren of St. Thomas Church in New York City . . .

* * *

Directory of Sources

Most of the resources noted in the foregoing pages will, it is hoped, be available through local book and record stores, public, parish, diocesan and/or university libraries. The following directory is included as an aid if close-to-hand sources should prove unproductive.

AMS Press, Inc.
56 E. 13th St.
New York, N.Y. 10003

Abingdon Press
201 Eighth Ave. S.
Nashville, Tenn. 37202

Agape Press
5705 W. Corcoran Place
Chicago, Ill. 60644

Appleton-Century-Crofts
440 Park Ave. S.
New York, N.Y. 10016

Augsburg Publishing House
426 S. Fifth St.
Minneapolis, Minn. 55415

BFA Educational Media
2211 Michigan Ave.
Santa Monica, Calif. 90404

A. S. Barnes & Co., Inc.
Forsgate Drive
Cranbury, N.J. 08512

Belwin Mills, Publisher
Rockville Center, N.Y. 11571

Boggs Academy
Keyesville, Ga. 30816

Boosey & Hawkes, Inc.
Bay Ave.
Oceanside, N.Y. 11572

Broadman Press
127 Ninth Ave., N.
Nashville, Tenn. 37234

C.S.S. Publishing Co.
628 S. Main St.
Lima, Ohio 45804

Caedmon Records, Inc.
505 Eighth Ave.
New York, N.Y. 10018

Chappell & Co., Inc.
609 Fifth Ave.
New York, N.Y. 10017

Chelsea House Publishers
70 W. 40th St.
New York, N.Y. 10018

Choristers Guild
P.O. Box 38188
Dallas, Tex. 75238

Clarabella Music, Ltd.
England (For U.S. contact see
Edward B. Marks Music Corp).

Cokesbury Bookstore
55 E. 55th St.
New York, N.Y. 10022

Columbia Records
45-20 83rd
Elmhurst (Flushing), N.Y. 11373

Cooperative Recreation
Services, Inc.
Delaware, Ohio 43015

Deutsche Grammophon/
Archive (See U.S. liaison,
International Music Consultants)

Doubleday & Co., Inc.
501 Franklin Ave.
Garden City, N.Y. 11530

John Day Company, Inc.
257 Park Ave. S.
New York, N.Y. 10010

E. P. Dutton & Co., Inc.
201 Park Ave. S.
New York, N.Y. 10003

Educational Audio-Visual, Inc.
17 Marble Ave.
Pleasantville, N.Y. 10570

Encyclopaedia Britannica Films
425 N. Michigan Ave.
Chicago, Ill. 60611

Extension Media Center
University of Southern Calif.
Berkeley, Calif. 94720

Eye Gate House, Inc.
146-01 Archer Ave.
Jamaica, N.Y. 11435

Folkways Records
701 Seventh Ave.
New York, N.Y. 10036

Follett Educational Corp.
1010 W. Washington Blvd.
Chicago, Ill. 60607

Fortress Press
2900 Queen Lane
Philadelphia, Pa. 19129

Friendship Press
475 Riverside Dr.
New York, N.Y. 10027

Galaxy Music Corp.
2121 Broadway
New York, N.Y. 10023

Galliard, Ltd.
Queen Anne's Road
Great Yarmouth, Norfolk
England (See U.S. liaison,
Galaxy Music Corp.)

Garrard Publishing Co.
1607 N. Market St.
Champaign, Ill. 61820

Gregorian Institute of America
2115 W. 63rd St.
Chicago, Ill. 60636

Grover-Jennings
P.O. Box 303
Monterey, Calif. 93940

Harcourt Brace Jovanovich, Inc.
757 Third Ave.
New York, N.Y. 10017

Hargail Music, Inc.
28 W. 38th St.
New York, N.Y. 10018

Harper & Row Publishers, Inc.
10 E. 53rd St.
New York, N.Y. 10022

John and Mary Harrell
P.O. Box 9006
Berkeley, Calif. 94709

Harvard University Press
79 Garden St.
Cambridge, Mass. 02138

Harvey House, Inc., Publishers
Irvington-on-Hudson, N.Y.
10533

Haydn Society Records
Esoterics, Inc.
P.O. Box 321
East Hartford, Conn. 06108

Hewitt House
Old Tappan, N.J. 07675

Holiday House, Inc.
18 E. 56th St.
New York, N.Y. 10022

Hope College
Holland, Mich. 49423

Hope Publishing Co.
Carol Stream, Ill. 60187

International Music Consultants
125 Park Ave.
New York, N.Y. 10017

Judson Press
Valley Forge, Pa. 19481

Alfred A. Knopf, Inc.
201 E. 50th St.
New York, N.Y. 10022

Kodály Musical Training
Institute
Wellesley Hills, Mass. 02181

J. B. Lippincott Co.
E. Washington Sq.
Philadelphia, Pa. 19105

Liturgical Conference
1330 Massachusetts Ave. N.W.
Washington, D.C. 20005

Lutheran Church Council
130 N. Wells St.
Chicago, Ill. 60606

Macmillan Publishing Co., Inc.
866 Third Ave.
New York, N.Y. 10022

Mark Custom Records
Keyesville, Ga. 30816

Edward B. Marks Music Corp.
136 W. 52nd St.
New York, N.Y. 10019

McGraw-Hill Book Co.
1221 Avenue of the Americas
New York, N.Y. 10020

W. W. Norton & Co., Inc.
55 Fifth Ave.
New York, N.Y. 10003

Pantheon Books
201 E. 50th St.
New York, N.Y. 10022

Paulist/Newman Press
1865 Broadway
New York, N.Y. 10023

Pflaum/Standard
38 W. Fifth St.
Dayton, Ohio 45402

Philips Records
(See International Music
Consultants)

Plenary Publications
International, Inc.
300 E. 40th St.
New York, N.Y. 10016

Plough Publishing House
Rifton, N.Y. 12471

Prentice-Hall, Inc.
Rte. 9
Englewood Cliffs, N.J. 07632

Proclamation Productions
Orange Square
Port Jervis, N.Y. 12771

G. P. Putnam's Sons
200 Madison Ave.
New York, N.Y. 10016

RCA Victor Records
RCA Educational Services
Camden, N.J. 08101

Random House, Inc.
201 E. 50th St.
New York, N.Y. 10022

Charles Scribners Sons
597 Fifth Ave.
New York, N.Y. 10017

Seabury Press, Inc.
815 Second Ave.
New York, N.Y. 10017

Silver Burdett
General Learning Corp.
250 James St.
Morristown, N.J. 07960

Simon and Schuster
630 Fifth Ave.
New York, N.Y. 10022

Small World Enterprises, Inc.
4716 Ellsworth Ave.
Pittsburgh, Pa. 15213

Sterling Publishing Co., Inc.
419 Park Ave. S.
New York, N.Y. 10016

Swann Motion Pictures
201 S. Jefferson Ave.
St. Louis, Mo. 63103

Teachers College Press
Columbia University
1234 Amsterdam Ave.
New York, N.Y. 10027

Tower Publications
185 Madison Ave.
New York, N.Y. 10016

Travarca
P.O. Box 247
Grandville, Mich. 49418

United Church Press
1505 Race St.
Philadelphia, Pa. 19102

University of Minnesota Press
2037 University Ave. S.E.
Minneapolis, Minn. 55455

Vanguard Records
71 W. 23rd St.
New York, N.Y. 10010

Van Nostrand-Reinhold Co.
450 W. 33rd St.
New York, N.Y. 10001

Viking Press, Inc.
625 Madison Ave.
New York, N.Y. 10022

Henry Z. Walck, Inc.
19 Union Square
New York, N.Y. 10003

Franklin Watts, Inc.
730 Fifth Ave.
New York, N.Y. 10019

Westminster Press
Witherspoon Bldg.
Philadelphia, Pa. 19107

Word, Inc.
4800 W. Waco Dr.
Waco, Tex. 76703

World Publishing Co.
110 E. 59th St.
New York, N.Y. 10022

Suppliers of Special Musical Instruments

Bird calls/reed horns/turntable whistles:

Magnamusic-Baton, Inc.
6390 Delmar Blvd.
St. Louis, Mo. 63130

(Studio 49, Orff Equipment)

Resonator bells/tone educator bells:

David Wexler & Co.
823 S. Wabash Ave.
Chicago, Ill. 60605

Toy harps/zithers/"Golden Junior Harp":

Try department stores, toy shops,
hobby shops, etc.